MAUDU'
A Way of Union with God

MAUDU'
A Way of Union with God

MUHAMMAD ADLIN SILA

PRESS

Published by ANU Press
The Australian National University
Acton ACT 2601, Australia
Email: anupress@anu.edu.au
This title is also available online at press.anu.edu.au

National Library of Australia Cataloguing-in-Publication entry

Creator: Sila, Muhammad Adlin, 1970- author.

Title: Maudu' : a way of union with God / Muhammad Adlin Sila.

ISBN: 9781925022704 (paperback) 9781925022711 (ebook)

Series: Islam in Southeast Asia.

Subjects: Muslims--Indonesia--Sulawesi Selatan.
Group identity--Indonesia--Sulawesi Selatan.
Ethnic groups--Indonesia--Sulawesi Selatan.
Islam--Indonesia--Sulawesi Selatan.
Sulawesi Selatan (Indonesia)--History.
Sulawesi Selatan (Indonesia)--Civilization.

Dewey Number: 305.800959847

All rights reserved. No part of this publication may be reproduced, stored in a retrieval system or transmitted in any form or by any means, electronic, mechanical, photocopying or otherwise, without the prior permission of the publisher.

Cover design and layout by ANU Press.

This edition © 2015 ANU Press

Islam in Southeast Asia Series

Theses at The Australian National University are assessed by external examiners and students are expected to take into account the advice of their examiners before they submit to the University Library the final versions of their theses. For this series, this final version of the thesis has been used as the basis for publication, taking into account other changes that the author may have decided to undertake. In some cases, a few minor editorial revisions have made to the work. The acknowledgements in each of these publications provide information on the supervisors of the thesis and those who contributed to its development. For many of the authors in this series, English is a second language and their texts reflect an appropriate fluency.

Contents

List of Illustrations...ix
List of Tables xi
A Note on Languages...xiii
Foreword xv
Abstract xvii

PART ONE
Introduction 3
1. The Scope of the Study 13
2. The *Lontara'*: The Bugis-Makassar Manuscripts and their Histories 27
3. Origin, Class Status and Socio-cultural Integration in Cikoang 41

PART TWO
4. The Ideological Dimensions of Disputes over
   Religious Practices in Cikoang 71
5. The Festivals of Maudu' and Pattumateang 91
6. Concluding Remarks 107

APPENDICES
I.   Types of *Lontara'*: The Bugis-Makassar Manuscripts 119
II. The Tale of the Three Datok 123
III. The Kinship Terms of the Cikoangese........................... 125
IV. Subdivisions of the Anakkaraeng 127
V.   The Ata, or Slaves, of South Sulawesi 129

Glossary... 131
Bibliography 137

List of Illustrations

Maps
The location of Desa Cikoang. 18

Figures
Figure 1: Portrait of Sayyid Jalaluddin al-'Aidid 35
Figure 2: The *sambulayang* indicates the social status of the house owner. . . . 54
Figure 3: Balla Lompoa, the house of a former Gowa ruler (Karaeng) 55
Figure 4: The house of the children of Karaeng (Anakkaraeng) 55
Figure 5: The house of distinguished people (Tubajik) 56
Figure 6: The house of commoners (Tusamarak). 56
Figure 7: The house of former slaves (Ata) 57
Figure 8: The playing of drums (*gandrang*) 57
Figure 9: The *kandawari* and *sulapa'* are put in a *bembengan*. 96
Figure 10: The *kandawari* are put on top of the *julung-julung* 97

Diagrams
Diagram 1: The transmission of Sayyid Descent 48
Diagram 2: Genealogy of H. Maluddin Daeng Sikki (a Sayyid Karaeng) 50
Diagram 3: Patrilineal descent 66

List of Tables

Table 1: Population of Cikoang by *lingkungan* and sex (1994). 17
Table 2: The names of Sayyid clans in Hadhramaut 22
Table 3: The genealogy of Sayyid Jalaluddin al-'Aidid 49
Table 4: Sayyid population by class and *lingkungan* in Cikoang. 53
Table 5: Sayyid population by class in Luar Batang hamlet,
  Kelurahan Penjaringan, North Jakarta, 1996. 73
Table 6: Kinship terms 126

A Note on Languages

The following abbreviations for languages cited in the study are as follows:

Ar.   Arabic, used not with diacritics, nor grammatically with case vowels or the singular and plural forms of nouns; rather, following Indonesian usage

Bug.   Buginese

In.   Indonesian

Mak.   Makassarese

For explanations of the terms used in this book, please see the Glossary.

Foreword

JAMES J. FOX

This is a study that calls for greater attention from a wider scholarly audience. It was originally submitted as a Master of Arts thesis in Asian Studies at The Australian National University (ANU) in 1998. It offers a fascinating case study of the Sayyid community of Cikoang in South Sulawesi – in particular, an examination of the role of the descendants of Sayyid Jalaluddin al-'Aidid, a Hadhrami merchant-teacher of great authority and charisma who is said to have initially settled in Gowa in the 17th century.

Whether Sayyid Jalaluddin came directly from Hadhramaut or by way of Aceh, when precisely he settled in Gowa, or why he moved to Cikoang and later to Sumbawa is unknown. Instead this study investigates the contemporary consequences of his appearance in Sulawesi and the establishment of the community of his descendants. It focuses on the Sayyid community in Cikoang, their historical intermarriage and cultural association with the Makassar nobility leading to the creation, among other things, of a title system that differentiates between Sayyid Karaeng, Sayyid Tuan and Sayyid Daeng who together comprise over two-thirds of the local community.

Sayyid Jalaluddin's legacy to the Cikoang community is the Tarekat Bahr ul-Nur whose mystic teachings expound the creation of the world from the 'Nur Muhammad.' A consequence of this teaching is an enormous emphasis on the celebration of Maudu' (Maulid, or the Birth of the Prophet) as expressed in the local assertion: 'My existence on this earth is for nothing but Maudu'.' Every year this prompts the Cikoang community to hold one of the most elaborate and colourful Maulid cerebrations in Indonesia.

If we are to appreciate the diverse historical sources of Islam in Indonesia, this is a study that deserves special attention.

For its author, Muhammad Adlin Sila, this study was a stepping stone to further research. He has now completed his PhD at ANU with a thesis, *Being Muslim in Bima of Sumbawa, Indonesia: Practice, Politics and Cultural Diversity*. This study of Bima and its religious history establishes him as a major researcher on the diverse traditions of Islam in eastern Indonesia.

The publication of this thesis is in line with the goal of the Islam in Southeast Asia series: to publish valuable research on Islam in Southeast Asia emanating from students at ANU.

There are two people who deserve special thanks in bringing this thesis to publication. The preparation of the manuscript from the original thesis was ably carried out by Dr Wendy Mukherjee who is a scholar of Indonesian Islam and a superb copyeditor. Dr Martin Slama, who is a scholar of the Hadhrami in Indonesia, played an important role in urging us to consider publishing this thesis.

Abstract

The village of Cikoang, situated on the south coast of South Sulawesi, Indonesia, is home to a community of Sayyid whose members trace their genealogical descent back to the Prophet Muhammad through their home in the Hadhramaut in southernmost Arabia. This is a study of how their identity is maintained both through kinship and marriage and through systems of belief and religious practices. The distinctiveness of the Sayyid of Cikoang is emphasised not only in their home village but also in places to which they have migrated, such as Kelurahan Penjaringan in Jakarta. This study explores the continuing strength of such an identity in contemporary Indonesia.

Kinship and marriage systems sustain the conviction of a bloodline that differentiates the Sayyid from other residents of Cikoang. Although marriages do occur between Sayyid and non-Sayyid, these are most usually between a Sayyid male and non-Sayyid female on the principle that children will inherit the descent status of their father. Sayyid women are compelled to marry only within the Sayyid community or to remain unmarried. A complex system of titles and status categories marks out different marriage arrangements entered into in the region.

Cikoang beliefs and religious practices, as enunciated by the Sayyid, persist despite the criticism of modernist Muslim groups in Indonesia, which are discussed in this study. Cikoang village members trace these practices to the words and actions of their founder, Sayyid Jalaluddin al-'Aidid, although they tend to justify them by reference to the Islamic scriptures of the Qur'an and the Hadith.

The Sayyid of Cikoang affirm the absolute oneness of God and strive to reach unity with Him within the gnosis of *ma'rifatullah*. The oneness of humanity and Allah, best exemplified in the persons of the Prophet Muhammad and his descendants, is enacted in Cikoang by the Sayyid through the celebration of the occasion of Maudu' or Maulid Nabi (Ar. the birth of the Prophet) and through

Pattumateang (Mak. the purification of deceased souls). These two rituals form the critical practices of the faith of the Sayyid. As well, the veneration of the Prophet and of later holy persons informs the theosophical doctrine of Bahr ul-Nur (Ar. The Sea of Light), the mystical order which they espouse. This is an order so far seldom treated in the study of Indonesian Sufism.

PART ONE

Introduction

The focus of the first part of this study is to discuss in a broader context the origins of the kinship system and religious identity of Hadhrami Sayyid Arabs in a *kampung* or *desa* (In. village) called Cikoang within the region of Makassar, South Sulawesi, Indonesia. Their system of marriage, employing the principle of *kafa'ah* (In. *sekufu* or *sepadan*, equality in partners) has made the Sayyid socially exclusive and at the same time rather different from other Indonesians. It lessens their flexibility (notably as concerns their womenfolk) in their assimilation with the local people. Although the Sayyid have lived in the area for a lengthy period, they have not become Makassarese in terms of titles, language, marriage policy and kinship system.

It is true that Arabs have lived in Indonesia for a long time and some have assimilated well with the local people. According to the Dutch scholar, L.W.C. Van den Berg, reporting in 1886, many of the Arabs and particularly their children were already difficult to distinguish from the local people: they were Indonesians. Partly because of the scarcity of women born in Arabia and Arab-born women who had been raised in the Hadhramaut, the Arabs in Indonesia tended to marry local women or women of Arab descent who had never been outside Indonesia.

As a consequence, the language spoken in the household of many Arabs was not Arabic but Indonesian, Javanese, Makassarese or other local languages of their womenfolk. They also used that language as the medium of communication with their children. The boys knew Arabic only as it was studied in their mostly religious-oriented schools. The girls knew a few Qur'anic verses for prayer.

The term 'Sayyid' or 'Arab' has always been associated with Islam in Indonesia. Since Islam originated in the land of Arabia, Indonesian Muslims often believe that religion and Arab race are one: the two are inseparable from one another.

Thus the day-to-day life of the Arabs should be an exemplary enactment of Islam and Indonesians tend to express surprise when Arabs do not always behave according to the main tenets of Islam.

Historically, it is believed that Arabs came to the archipelago of Indonesia even before Islam was born in Arabia in the 7th century. An Arab presence is known in the Indonesian region prior to the 16th century, the 'early Islamic period' there, partly for reasons of trade (see Van den Berg 1886; Tibbets 1957; and Meglio 1970; cf. Algadri 1984) and partly in order to spread the faith.

There is still controversy among scholars about the wider question of who first brought Islam to Indonesia. Some authorities point to Muslim traders from Persia and Gujarat; others offer evidence of direct Arab influences, either from the Hejaz or the Hadhramaut, on early Indonesian Muslims. But everyone agrees that Islam entered Indonesia peacefully without holy wars or rebellions.

Van den Berg (1886) declared that Islam set down its roots in Indonesia primarily due to the endeavours of Arabs and not of Indians. Even Van den Berg found it was naive to imagine that all Arabs were devoted Muslims, because in reality many were transgressors of the teachings of Islam. They were like ordinary Indonesian Muslims, both good and bad.

One recent study by Hamid Algadri (1984) postulated that it was Christiaan Snouck Hurgronje, political adviser to the colonial government and successor to Van den Berg, who was most responsible for preventing the assimilation of Indonesian Arabs with the local people. According to Algadri, Snouck Hurgronje's main duty was to preserve the 'divide and rule' politics of colonialism in the region. Snouck Hurgronje (1906) believed that the Arabs, with their close association with religion, were the main threat to Dutch power. Therefore their further assimilation and influence was to be prevented. Snouck Hurgronje noted that the various internal clashes that occurred between Dutch local authorities and Indonesians in a number of regions during the colonial period were in fact inspired and pioneered by Arab-born people; for example, the 30-year Aceh War, the longest ever experienced by the Dutch, was led by Habib Abdurrahman az-Zahir, a Sayyid.

So the understanding of the Arabs' religious orientation at present is in part a result of Hurgronje's legacy (Algadri 1984; Bowen 1993); for example, the Indonesians themselves often see the Arab Muslims as different. People refer to them as *orang-orang keturunan Arab Islam* (In. those of Muslim Arab descent) rather than simply Muslims. They are credited to be different in character and disposition from Indonesian Muslims. Similarly, the Makassarese differentiate the Makassar Arabs from themselves though both communities are Muslim. It seems that the fact of being of another country of origin implies a separate understanding of religious adherence.

In the second part of this study, I discuss religious arguments arising between Cikoangese traditionalist Muslims, who hold to the practice of a certain tradition of *tasawuf* (In. mystical discipline) pioneered by the Sayyid and the Muhammadiyah, the largest reform organisation of Indonesia. The latter encourages Muslims to perform rituals only as prescribed by the main sources of Islam, the Qur'an and Hadith and those ratified by Shariah, the laws of Islam. It will emerge in my discussion that there are clear distinctions between *tasawuf* and Shariah in debates by the two parties. Each side claims itself to be the only true practitioners of Islamic teachings.

According to the people of Cikoang, *tasawuf*, or Sufism, is a particular form of knowledge with regard to Allah. *Ma'rifatullah* (Ar. Islamic gnosis or genuine spirituality) is to be regarded as the central and the most vital part of all religions. *Ma'rifatullah* is a perfect way of worship based on love, not out of fear of the punishments of hell, nor on hope of the rewards of paradise. It is a way of understanding the inner facts of religion rather than its outward and perceptible form. It is a recognised subject matter in Islamic studies, which deals with methods to gain proximity to Allah, although certain of its practices may be at odds with 'true' Islamic teachings within the perspective of religious modernists.

In expressing their love towards Allah and hoping to gain *Ma'rifatullah*, the Cikoangese celebrate a Maulid Nabi festival, locally called Maudu' (Ar. both referring to the birthday of the Prophet Muhammad), each year. The same festival gives veneration to the Prophet and his descendants, the Sayyid.

The Prophet Muhammad is conceived of as the best Sufi master, who lived out Sufistic doctrines in his sayings and his deeds. He has said: 'Whoever knows himself will know Allah.' When a man, desiring to remember Allah alone comes to know that the only path of perfect guidance is that of knowing himself: he understands that his true guide is Allah alone. He forsakes all other paths. *Tasawuf*, or Sufism, is that way of purifying the heart. Its main objective is to find the key of nearness to Allah. In this undertaking humans should cleanse their hearts from any harmful influences. Since Allah is both the origin and destination of humankind, and of all other creatures, the interests of Allah must supervene before those of humans. Sufism is a total submission to Allah, while the Shariah, encompassing a set of social and material practices, is only the means applied in the process of submission. The Shariah is likened to the medium of transportation to the destination, and not the final goal of submission to Allah.

Those who stand for Shariah will certainly oppose these ideas because in their point of view all activities engaged in by humans are also, in principle, a form of submission to Allah. People work in order to earn money for the sustenance of their family and that, too, is an act of obedience to Allah. Humans need not leave their worldly activities entirely, as long as their doings are intended to win Allah's mercy. The least that humans can do is to curb themselves in their material or immoral desires, yet without wholly alienating themselves from worldly pursuits.

For the Sufis on the other hand, Sufism is spiritual training to acquire the essence of worshipping Allah. Without Sufism, the worship of Allah is mere obligation. Sufism teaches its practitioners how to perform the religious duties, such as prayer, with joy and pleasure. A state of ecstasy is achieved when the practitioners finally communicate directly with Allah, since they see Him wherever and whenever they perform prayer.

As elsewhere in its history, Sufism has played a major role in proselytising among common Indonesians. It has been intrinsic to Islam in the region. The local people embraced the belief of the oneness of a supernatural entity – the essentiality of the Sufistic doctrine. Islam and the Sufi teachers, together with Muslim traders (mostly Arabs and Sayyid), were welcomed by the local people. Arabs came to be seen as the sole religious teachers to new converts to Islam and especially to aspirants to Sufism. This placed them among the most respected strata of Indonesian society.

Many more of the early Sufi teachers or masters who had reached the highest spiritual stations were not native Indonesians. They were foreigners from Saudi Arabia, the Hadhramaut, India, Persia and elsewhere. They came to the Indonesian archipelago – first to Sumatra, Java, then Sulawesi; many of them married and stayed until the end of their lives, while some returned home after they had completed their mission.

It was the custom of Sufis to travel from one place to another in search of accomplished masters, or to find students to listen to their teachings, following the routes set by the Muslim traders. By the time Islam became the major religion of Indonesia, most Sufi masters were native Indonesians or descendants from intermarriage between Indonesians and outsiders who lived in Indonesia.

A Sufi master is certified to teach Sufism to seekers or students, to teach them how to purify themselves, to improve morality and to strengthen their inner and outer life (these three being the main teachings of Sufism) in order to attain perpetual bliss. First, the masters concentrated on building up the consciousness of their followers in the belief in the true Creator of this universe. Then they guided them in how to worship God through the Shariah: thus it can be said that Sufism preceded Shariah.

A Sufi master not only teaches the theory of Sufism to his disciples, but also works on their spiritual side, guiding them towards a higher degree of understanding of the truth of life. In return, seekers must follow a master able to guide them in the way of Allah and to illuminate that way for them until the state of true subjection is reached. The seekers must swear an oath of allegiance and promise their guide to leave their bad manners and habits in order to lift themselves to a better conduct in order to reach the perfect knowledge of spirituality.

Yet not all Sufi masters have disciples; some of them do not teach at all. On the other hand, not all teachers within Sufism are masters; most are still seekers themselves. True Sufi masters are very rare. It is said that to meet one is like finding a precious diamond among common pebbles. In 17th-century Gowa, among the best-known masters were Syekh Abdul Fattah Abu Yahya Abdul Bashir Adh-Dhariri Ar-Rafani and the popular Syekh Yusuf Tajul Khalwati Al-Makassari, founder of a chapter of the Tarekat Naqsyabandi-Khalwatiyah. The majority of the people of South Sulawesi adhere to this latter order (Hamid 1994).

During the 20th century, Sufism endured in the face of criticism put forward by various movements such as that of the largest Indonesian Muslim organisations, the traditionalist Nahdhatul Ulama, (NU, The Revival of Religious Scholars) and the modernist Muhammadiyah (lit. 'that which is pertaining or attributable to the Prophet Muhammad'). There were other anti-Sufi movements and even internal challenges mounted by modern forms of Sufism. Sufism was once declared to be the main cause of the deterioration and backwardness of the Muslim community throughout the world. It was also said that Sufism had made a historical distortion of the teachings of Islam, isolating its followers from proper social interaction by its application of contemplative disciplines. The criticism today of the Sufis is that they are old-fashioned traditionalists who oppose progress and modernity.

Among the chief fault-finders of Sufism worldwide are the *fuqaha*, the experts in Islamic jurisprudence, and the *mutakallim*, or theologians. These groups believe that Islam needs purification from corrupting influences and practices, and call for a reformulation of doctrine in the light of modern thought. In doing so, they believe that the conditions of Muslims will be improved and their understanding will be enlightened through both the religious and the secular sciences (cf. Adams 1933: 110). The modernists may also regard Sufism as having been influenced by other mystical sects from outside Islam, such as in Hinduism, Neo-Platonism and Christian asceticism.

The essence of Sufism lies in a belief in the unification of man and Allah called *wahdat al-wujud* (Ar. the unity of being) ascribed to the Andalusian Master Ibn al-Arabi (1165–1240). This concept of unification is inevitably seen to resemble Hindu *Vedanta* philosophy (Woodward 1989: 215). Sufi spiritual training also imitates or copies that of other domains of belief, such as the application of breath control, meditation and fasting – all also to be found in Hindu yoga. Such are the chief points of contact between Sufism and the mystical practices of other religions.

Such various stereotyped characteristics of Sufism are actually not universal, however, because in fact not all *tarekat* or orders teach that it is necessary to leave worldly things in order to attain the key of nearness to Allah, as is believed by the modernists. If we review the teachings of Syekh Yusuf Tajul Khalwati, the founder of the Tarekat Khalwatiyah (lit. Way of Seclusion) in South Sulawesi and Banten, West Java, we find the main tenets of a moderate Sufi doctrine. Syekh Yusuf insisted that this worldly life should not be totally abandoned and carnal desire must not be eliminated completely, but rather that this present human life should become the means to draw close to Allah.

However, the flaring up of desires to pursue worldly temptations is to be controlled through a set of exercises which strengthen self-discipline for the sake of Allah. The condition of carnal desire must always be checked and maintained so that it will not smother the vital organ of *qalbu* from its spiritual capability. In Arabic, *qalbu* means 'heart, soul or mind' (cf. Nicholson 1921: 113). It is the place where all knowledge about transcendental truth is cultivated. By knowing his or her *qalbu*, the seeker will know him or herself and lead to the recognition of Allah, the Creator. This is well illustrated in the oft-quoted stanza from among the poems of Hamzah Fansuri, the famed Sufi of Barus in 16th-century North Sumatra:

> *Hamzah Fansuri di dalam Makkah*
> *Mencari Tuhan di bait al-Ka'bah*
> *Di Barus ke Qudus terlalu payah*
> *Akhirnya dapat di dalam rumah* (XXI, 14)
> (Drewes and Brakel 1986: 108)

The interpretation of which runs as follows:

> Hamzah Fansuri, while at Mecca
> Sought God in the shrine of the Ka'ba
> Barus to Jerusalem is a journey too far
> He found Him within his own house at last

And the last line of which refers to the inner 'house', the *qalbu*.

The spiritual seeker cannot recognise the existence of Allah and submit to His will unless the *qalbu* is guarded from domination by worldly desires. The Sufis agree that the only way to grasp the key of nearness to Allah is through the purification of the *qalbu*, for it is said to be the locus and generator of *iman*, or faith, and not of rationality. Like other Sufi masters, Syekh Yusuf Khalwati observed Islam in its two aspects, the external (*lahiriah*) and the internal (*bathiniah*) – Shariah, the observance of the law, being the external aspect of Islam and Sufism its internal aspect. Shariah produces the guidelines for performing rituals and conducting daily life, whereas Sufism generates their essence, the two should be applied together. Without minimising the role of the Shariah, the deepening of Sufism, which produces *haqiqah* (Ar. divine truth, reality) is the more emphasised. Internal experience can be obtained through performing the religious practices set out by the law. Thus Sufism without Shariah is invalid and Shariah without Sufism is pointless (Hamid 1994: 157–158). Syekh Yusuf taught that we should see both Sufism and Syari'at as one totality in the path to obtain *ma'rifatullah*.

Recent phenomena in Indonesia attest that there has been a growing interest among Indonesians to study Sufism. Sufism is now open to everyone, without the fear of being branded 'traditionalist'. The Muslims of Cikoang have a new appreciation of Sufism and of the religious legitimacy of the Sayyid as teachers of Sufism in modern times. As an overall trend, Sufism has won a place among the urban people of Indonesia as well. It no longer belongs solely to rural traditionalists.

Muslims living in Jakarta, for example, who are usually described as urban, modern and progressive are now regularly attending private courses in Sufism provided by at least three established institutions: Yayasan Tazkiyah Sejati (The Sejati Spiritual Foundation), founded by the Sri Adyanti B.N. Rachmadi, the daughter of the former Vice-President Sudharmono and now directed by Jalaluddin Rakhmat or 'Kang Jalal'; Yayasan Barzakh (The Barzakh Foundation); and Yayasan Wakaf Paramadina (The Paramadina Charitable Foundation) (*Inside Indonesia*, Edition No. 52 October 1997, *Tiras*, Edition No. 52/26 January 1998, and *Ummat*, Edition No. 9/15 September 1997).

Paramadina was founded in 1986 by a number of Muslim businessmen and intellectuals. Among them, Nurcholish Madjid, or 'Cak Nur', a prominent liberal Muslim scholar, has offered several packages of courses on Sufism in the last several years. Previously, religious courses facilitated by this foundation covered general studies of Islam such as Kalam, theology (*fiqih*), jurisprudence, Islamic history (*sejarah Islam*), and now *tasawuf* has been added. The latter has proved to be the most popular course among urban audiences.

The rising popularity of Sufism represents a new phase in the life of Islam in Indonesia. It is the direct consequence of a shift in the political system to favour Islam since the end of Suharto's New Order in 1989 (see Hefner 1993; Liddle 1996; Fealy 1997). Many state policies have benefited the Indonesian Muslims under this period of *Reformasi*. More and more devout Muslims are occupying high-ranking posts in the bureaucracy. The alliance between Angkatan Bersenjata Republik Indonesia (ABRI), the Indonesian Armed Forces and Islam is becoming more apparent. The establishment of Ikatan Cendekiawan Muslim Indonesia (ICMI; Indonesian Association of Muslim Intellectuals) and Bank Muamalat, a banking system based on Shariah, is another breath of fresh air for Indonesian Muslims. Religious meetings regularly take place, at any time and anywhere, without the requirement to ask for government permission. Many Indonesians believe this is a time of victory for Muslims.

This condition of freedom to express their Islamic piety publicly has led Muslims into other kinds of pursuits of a more comprehensive knowledge of Islam. Kelompok Pengajian Keagamaan (religious study groups) are mushrooming in offices, hotels and other luxurious sites. Books on Shariah, Kalam and Sufism sell well. Discussions about obligatory and optional religious practices are increasingly becoming part of everyday discourse. Today, Indonesian Muslims seem to welcome all kinds of Islamic orientations, as long as their thirst for religious knowledge is met.

What needs to be stressed is that this religious phenomenon has spread more openly among the Indonesian elite. A number of top officials in the bureaucracy – businessmen, executives and other high wage earners – are now affiliating themselves with Sufism. Anderson, as recorded by local mass media (e.g. *Tiras*, No. 52/26 January 1998) maintains that this is a recent development. It would seem that an over-abundance of material wealth in these times of new prosperity has led many to a state of existential emptiness, prompting them to search for the meaning of life. They no longer indulge themselves in food and drink, because the basic needs are already well satisfied. They no longer compete for promotion. They turn to study Sufism, yet without excluding their worldly activities altogether.

Another trend is that not everyone is serious in studying Sufism as an intellectual discipline. For some people Sufism is an escape from the unpredictability of their future. Life is full of uncertainty. Political downfall and loss of wealth can happen at any time. Under such conditions, there are many who feel anxious and suffer mental stress, turning to Sufism in the pursuit of tranquillity.

We consider this phenomenon to be modern Sufism, or 'popular' Sufism. For example, businessmen can still run their businesses while practising Sufism. The impact has been in a change of attitudes toward wealth. Frequent donations are made to humanitarian causes. Judged from the yardstick of traditional asceticism, this is the concept of social Sufism, promoting good deeds. The teachings of Sufism which emphasise the social dimension of humanity come to the fore. Every Muslim, regardless of his or her religious orientation and adherence, can now affiliate himself or herself with Sufism.

This new Sufism comes with a different face and is completely different from that in Cikoang. There is in it neither a veneration of holy persons (saints, teachers, Sayyid families) nor extensive celebrations of the Prophet Muhammad's birthday as a means to obtain union with Allah. It is to the study of such 'traditional' Sufism in South Sulawesi that we turn to now.

CHAPTER ONE

The Scope of the Study

Objectives

This study examines questions of the historical origins and religious distinctiveness of a community in Kampung Cikoang, Takalar Regency on the south coast in the southern part of South Sulawesi. Cikoang has a population of about 8,000 people, ranked in an elaborate social hierarchy. It is in most respects a typical village in a region where all people speak the Turatea dialect of Makassarese.[1]

The inhabitants of Kampung Cikoang claim to be Sunni Muslims following Shafi'i jurisprudence and sharing a common historical tradition. Their distinctive religious practices are the celebration of Maudu' or Maulid Nabi (Ar., In. the Birth of the Prophet Muhammad) and Pattumateang (Mak. the Purification of Dead Souls).

Social stratification is an important feature of this community. The people of Cikoang belong to one of two social strata. The first is that of the Arab Sayyid[2] who claim to be descendants of the Prophet through the al-'Aidid family of the Hadhramaut. They are often the *anrongguru* (Mak.) or religious specialists and teachers of the area. Sayyid is an Arabic term and the equivalent of *tuan*, or master, in Indonesian. The term Syarif meaning 'honourable' is also used while the feminine forms, Syarifah and Sayyidah refer to a lady of a Sayyid house.

---

1   There are three chief dialects in Makassarese: Lakiung, Turatea (predominantly used in Takalar and Jeneponto regions) and Konjo (mostly found in Selayar Regency, Tamaona and Tabbinjai villages). See also Daeng Patunru 1983 and Mattulada 1982.
2   Nurdin et al. 1977/1978: 16–20; Hisyam 1985. See also Van den Berg 1886.

The title of Sayyid is normally attributed to the descendants of the Prophet from his grandson, Husein, the son of Ali and Fatimah, the Prophet's daughter, while Syarif refers to the descent of Hasan, their elder son.[3]

The second social stratum of Cikoang is that of the Jawi or the non-Sayyid. This word is perhaps derived from the Javanese term *jawa*, referring to the Javanese people and to Indonesians in general. As an Arabic word, *jawiiun* was used to refer to Indonesian pilgrims who went to Mecca in the 19th century and settled there, most of whom were Javanese.[4] Thus, the term Jawi for the non-Sayyid people in Cikoang might have been introduced by the Sayyid themselves to identify the local people as non-Arabs.

The Sayyid system of Cikoang is based unequivocally on descent. The strata are mutually exclusive and recruitment is by birth alone. Members of each stratum have specific attributes and roles which differentiate them from members of the other stratum. These differences are most obvious in the realms of religion and tradition. The social fabric of Kampung Cikoang is discussed further in Chapter Three.

Due to their prestigious descent, the Sayyid appear to have more power than the Jawi. Historically, they have been authorities over the Jawi people, particularly in religious and traditional terms (Hisyam 1985: 54) which has led the Cikoangese to be involved in a patron–client relationship structure. With their religious and traditional legitimacy, the Sayyid have positioned themselves as the patrons.

In the first part of this study, therefore, it has been necessary to examine the historical data of the coming of the Sayyids' ancestor, Sayyid Jalaluddin al-'Aidid, and his children to South Sulawesi and their first assimilation with the local people in Kampung Cikoang. Historical research into the relationship between the Arab countries of the Middle East and the Cikoangese is not the basic aim here, however.[5] Other scholars have done this and I merely recount the results of their research.[6] Nor are my own findings about the role of Islamisation in South Sulawesi intended to challenge observations made by others; rather, my aim is to give a more concrete specification of the regional orientations of

---

[3] Ahmad 1976: 15. For a different interpretation see Abaza 1988: 6, in which both the Sayyid and the Syarif claim to be the descendants of Husein.

[4] Information derived from the research of C. Snouck Hurgronje, who visited Mecca in the 19th century as a pilgrim in order to observe the activities of the thousands of pilgrims coming from the East Indies (Noer 1973: 33; Hisyam 1985).

[5] Historians argue whether it was the Hadhramis who introduced Islam into Indonesia or if Hadhrami migration is primarily an 18th-century phenomenon. It is accepted that the principal intermediaries of Islam in earlier centuries were from South India and from the Hejaz.

[6] See Nurdin et al. 1977/1978; Hamonic 1985: 178; Pelras 1985: 113; Van den Berg 1886; Gervais 1971; Abaza 1988; Noorduyn 1956a: 247–266; Mattulada 1976; Algadri 1984, 1994; Hamid 1994. See also Bujra 1971 and Chelhod 1984 for many other local sources.

Islam in South Sulawesi, and particularly in Cikoang. This objective also allows for a more detailed description of unpublished religious phenomena among the Sayyid traditions of Makassar through my ethnographic analysis.

Since the descendants of Sayyid Jalaluddin al-'Aidid reside not only in Cikoang, but also in other parts of Indonesia, this study is focused on three regions – Cikoang, Ujung Pandang and Jakarta – and is the result of four months of fieldwork in those areas in 1996–1997.

The study is divided into two parts. In Chapter Two I shall recount the coming of Islam to South Sulawesi in general and the coming of Sayyid Jalaluddin to Cikoang in particular through an exploration of Bugis-Makassar manuscripts (Mak. *lontara'*) in conjunction with traditional stories handed down by the elders (Mak. *caritana turioloa*).

In Chapter Three I explore the framework of the historical origins of the Sayyid, especially after the coming of Sayyid Jalaluddin. I analyse the implications of the origins of the Sayyid in terms of socio-religious patterns and the development of Kampung Cikoang, especially in terms of hierarchy and alliance, origin, status level and socio-cultural integration, as well as of their marriage practices.

The second part of the study discusses the religious understanding of the Cikoangese as a whole – Sayyid and Jawi – in comparison to that of other Muslims in Indonesia. In Chapter Four my main concern is to explore a framework which will elucidate the differences in the Islamic practices between the Cikoangese (Mak. *tu Cikoang*; In. *orang Cikoang*) and the non-Cikoangese, or outsiders (Mak. *tu pantara*; In. *orang luar*). This leads in Chapter Five into a discussion of the extent to which the two groups of Muslims propose different methods of the 'proper' conduct of religious rituals, the Maudu' and Pattumateang in particular.

I shall give an account of the Maudu' and Pattumateang rites from a Cikoangese perspective and examine elements of those practices which outsiders, notably members of the Muslim reformist organisation Muhammadiyah, do not agree with. These outsiders are mostly non-Cikoangese, but there may be some Cikoangese among them. Finally, in Chapter Six, a tentative conclusion is put forward about the historical origins and religious identity of the Sayyid. This chapter also presents a number of critical aspects of the study that call for further research in the future.

Review of the literature

The existence of the Sayyid in Cikoang with their distinctive practices of Maudu' and Pattumateang have been an integral part of the Makassarese historical context for centuries. Their long-standing presence has attracted discussions by both Indonesian and non-Indonesian scholars alike. Nevertheless, such studies have been based on inadequate data regarding the historical origins and religious distinctiveness of the Sayyid. For instance, Nurdin and his colleagues carried out research in 1977/1978. They provided a sophisticated report on the Maudu' in Cikoang, through which a general understanding of the Cikoangese as a whole became available to other researchers. However, their account simply provides a description of the ceremonies according to the view of local practitioners without any comparison to similar practices conducted by Muslims elsewhere. Such a comparison, to me, is necessary in order to show how distinct the Cikoangese rite is.

Similarly, the sociologist Muhammad Hisyam (1985) observed the social networks between the Sayyid and Jawi people. One of his findings was that the Sayyid and Jawi exercise patron–client relations which form a set of reciprocal practices. Hisyam also discussed the reciprocal relationship between *anrongguru*, or teachers, and *ana'guru*, or students, within the religious domain. The *anrongguru* are in charge of giving religious teaching while the *ana'guru* are obligated to give goods and other necessities to the *anrongguru* in return (see further Chapter Four). Unfortunately, Hisyam's account lacks an elaboration of the content of religious teachings taught by the *anrongguru* and this study attempts to meet that deficiency.

We also find well-documented information about the fundamentals of conducting Maudu' in Cikoang in the account given by Gilbert Hamonic (1985). Hamonic found that some of the Cikoangese beliefs and practices have their roots in the doctrines of Shi'ism. He also stressed the point that the Maudu' is a distinctive ceremony among the Cikoangese passed on by their elders (see Chapters Four and Five). Finally, despite a broad discussion of the Islamisation of South Sulawesi, Christian Pelras (1985) only devoted a few lines to the coming of Sayyid Jalaluddin al-'Aidid as the initiator of that Islamisation and as the founder of the Sayyid community of Cikoang.

The area of Cikoang

Kampung Cikoang is situated in the southern part of Takalar Regency. The village is in the shape of a rectangle, with Jeneponto Regency to the east, Lakatong village to the northwest and Laikang village to the south (see maps on page 18 of this volume). Within Cikoang there are four *lingkungan*, or hamlets: Lingkungan Cikoang, Pattopakkang, Bontoparang and Panjangkalang. For the purpose of this study, I consider the main *lingkungan* of Cikoang and the other three as one social unit and the name Cikoang will be used to refer to this unit as a whole.

Table 1: Population of Cikoang by *lingkungan* and sex (1994)

Lingkungan (hamlet)	Male	Female	Number
1. Cikoang	1.096	1.404	2,500
2. Pattopakkang	961	1.070	2,031
3. Bontoparang	932	994	1,926
4. Panjangkalang	887	956	1,843
Total	3,876	4,424	8,300
Per cent	46.7	53.3	100.0

Source: *Cikoang Dalam Angka* 1994 (as cited from Achmad 1995).

Table 1 gives a breakdown of the population of each *lingkungan*, in which Lingkungan Cikoang is shown to be the most populous. Kampung Cikoang, which covers 20 square kilometres, is located in the *kecamatan*, or district, of Mangarabombang, Takalar Regency. The people depend for their subsistence on salt making and agriculture (90 per cent) and fishing (10 per cent). The main product is salt, approximating 3,000 to 4,000 tonnes per year.[7] Houses are built close to each other near the river and in a very Makassar style of construction, *balla rate* (In. *rumah panggung*) or stilted houses. Table 1 also indicates that females outnumber males in all of Cikoang – at the time of my collecting of data I had not discovered the social or cultural reasons to account for this.

---

7   See Hisyam 1985: 14. The business of salt-making is centred in northern Lingkungan Cikoang and Pattopakang. Activity runs in the dry season, lasting for four to five months. When the rainy seasons begins, the Cikoangese resume farming. Achmad 1995 provides a more recent detailed description of the subsistence of the Cikoangese.

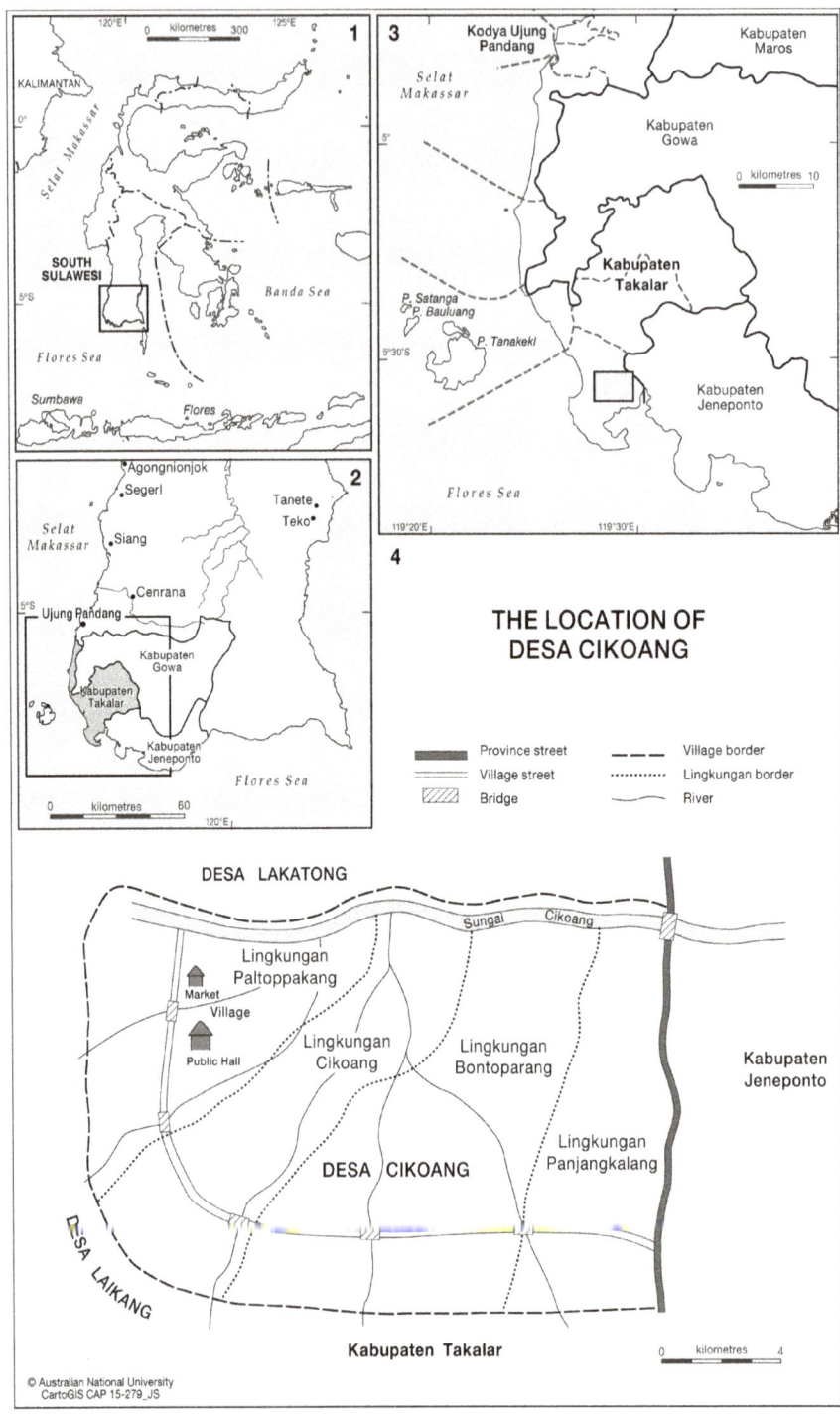

Maps: The location of Desa Cikoang
Map 1: South Sulawesi; Map 2: Takalar Regency; Map 3: Takalar Regency; Map 4: Desa Cikoang
Source: ANU CartoGIS.

According to the records of Cikoang, a nobleman called Karaeng Cikondong from Binamu (in Jeneponto Regency) first founded Cikoang in around 1514 (Hamonic 1985). With 44 loyal followers, he opened up new land by clearing forest and giving the settlement its name.[8] At the time, this settlement was counted in the village of Laikang to the south. Basing his assertions on a local source, Hisyam (1985) notes that in the last years of the 16th century, Laikang had grown to become a small autonomous kingdom. Its first ruler was a Bugis prince named Makkasaung ri Langi', who was the son of Arumpone Petta Punggawa, king of the kingdom of Bone. He was appointed the ruler of Laikang. Makkasaung ri Langi' then married the daughter of one of the Laikang nobility. From this union, Makkarausu Daeng Ngilau was born, who then replaced his father as the ruler of Laikang. This tiny kingdom persisted until the early 20th century.[9]

Like other people of Makassar in the past, the Cikoangese were known as great seafarers. From their strategic position of Cikoang located on the south coast of South Sulawesi, they came into contact through sea trade with other ethnic communities of Indonesia such as the Acehnese and Malays, who were already in the main Muslims. According to local historians, Islam most likely put down its roots in Cikoang due to the commercial relationship between the Cikoangese and the Muslim world (Hisyam 1985).

The coming of Islam to Cikoang in the first years of the 17th century is traditionally associated with an Acehnese *ulama*, an Islamic scholar, genealogically descended from the Hadhramaut by name of Jalaluddin, a Sayyid of the al-'Aidid clan (Hisyam 1985). It is due to his efforts that today all the people of Cikoang are Muslims and most respect the traditions of the Sayyid in their socio-religious life. Before establishing Islam in Cikoang, Jalaluddin and his family made a sojourn to the South Sulawesi kingdom of Gowa where he had been invited by Datok ri Bandang, one of the early fathers of Islamisation in South Sulawesi, to help spread religion in the region (see Nurdin et al. 1977/1978). Thus Jalaluddin also played a part in the establishment of Islam in South Sulawesi in general, following the rulers of the kingdoms of Gowa and Tallo' (1603–1605) (Mattulada 1976: 19).

---

8   He purchased the land by paying the ruler of the kingdom of Gowa 40 water buffaloes, see Hamonic 1985.
9   In 1996, based on a decree by provincial authority No 450/XII.1965, the term *desa* was issued. After that Laikang was divided into two, Desa Cikoang and Desa Laikang (cf. Hisyam 1985: 126).

Historical accounts also tell that the early Arab presence in Indonesia was undoubtedly related to sea trade along the route to China.[10] Most Indonesianists, both Indonesian and non-Indonesian, also believe that ports in Gujarat on the southwest corner of Rajputana, India had long been important centres of commercial and religious relations between East and the West as well. Foreign traders – Arabs, Persians, Chinese and Indonesians – regularly frequented the Gujarati harbour town of Cambay, for example (Gibb 1957: 228–229).

It was due to the efforts of these Muslim merchants, Arabs, Indians, Persians or Chinese, that Islam took root in Indonesia (Ali 1970; Patji 1991). From India must have come the influence of the Shi'ah variant of Islam, of which traces are still found in Java and the Minangkabau area of Sumatra, whose Tabut ceremony commemorates the death of the Prophet's grandson Husein. According to historians, Muslim traders on the route to China regularly visited certain ports in Southeast Asia from the 7th or 8th century, but Islamic kingdoms as centres of power only became established from the 13th century. This assumption is the most popular and is commonly used by most Indonesianists. It is based on a report of Marco Polo, the Venetian traveller who visited Aceh in 1292. He wrote:

> The people of Perlec (Perlak) used all to be idolaters but owing to contact with Saracen merchants, who continually resort here in their ships, they have all been converted to the law of Muhammad. This applies only to the inhabitants of the city (Zainuddin 1968: 60; cf. Patji 1991: 27).

Adopting Marco Polo's account, it is generally accepted that the first Muslim communities in Indonesia date from the 13th century (see Drewes 1968: 443; Johns 1980: 165; Atjeh 1985).[11] From the 13th to the 15th centuries, there was a close trading exchange between Southern Arabia (especially Muskat and the Hadhramaut), the Hejaz, Egypt, the East African coast, China, India and Indonesia (Berg 1886: 1, 67; Arnold 1913: 363–407; Reid 1988, 1993) giving opportunities to Arab traders to set up settlements in many important ports in Indonesia.

According to Van den Berg (1886: 67–68) Arab traders had long been in Indonesia but their numbers were relatively small until the late 18th century. In 1812–1813, their total number in Java and Madura were only 621, coming under the

---

10 Haji Agus Salim maintains that, according to an Arab historian, the Arab vessels used to sail along the sea shores of the South Indian Ocean to the Nicobar Islands and then past the northern part of Sumatra to Kedah and through the Straits of Malacca. Their route then branched out in two directions: either northwards to China or eastwards to Palembang or Java. Usually they first went eastwards then north, past Cambodia and Cochinchina to China. Thus it was no wonder that the Arabs, Persians and Indians (Muslims from the West) knew Indonesia and its people from the earliest times when they began to bring their merchandise to the East. Agus Salim concluded that at that time no ships except those of the Muslims carried maritime commerce through the Indian Ocean (Kraemer and Nieuwenhuijze 1952: 112–113; cf. Ali 1970, *The Spread of Islam in Indonesia*, Yayasan NIDA, Yogyakarta.
11 e.g. the grave of Sultan Malik as-Saleh in Pasai, North Sumatra, dated 1297.

designation of *'orang Arab Moro'* (Arab Muslims).[12] Later, the figure increased steadily with an influx of new immigrants from the Hadhramaut. This was due to the improvement of sea transportation with the opening of the Suez Canal, steam shipping and the concomitant development of economic possibilities.[13]

The Sayyid in Indonesia are historically believed to have emigrated from the Hadhramaut (Berg 1886; Abaza 1988).[14] This region of Southern Arabia enjoyed an abundant history of religious and intellectual life. The Hadhramis were known as sophisticated people, hard-working traders, intellectuals and saints or holy men (Berg 1886) and were particularly predominant in spreading the Shafi'i school of Sunni law (Serjeant 1981, VIII 25; Bujra 1971; Berg 1886).[15] Renaud (1984: 57) argues, however, that the Zaydi doctrine[16] of an early Shi'ite sect (one of whose identifying characteristics is that their *imam* must be a descendant of the Prophet) was spread and developed in parts of Yemen during the 12th century. Nevertheless, Zaydism is closer to Sunni Islam than Indian Isma'ilism or the Shi'i profession of Iran. The majority of Yemenis adhere to the Shafi'i school. It was therefore probably the Hadhramis, along with other Sunni Muslim immigrants, who brought with them Shafi'ism, which has become the predominant law school of Indonesian Muslims at large.

Despite the fact that all Hadhramis speak the same variant of Arabic and belong to the same stream of religion, there exists social stratification among them. Four major hierarchical strata were recognised,[17] as follows: the Sayyid; the Mashayekh (sing. Sheikh);[18] the Kaba'il; the tradespeople; and the Masakin

---

12 See also Raffles 1817: 6, table lists 430 people for Batavia and 168 for Pekalongan; cf. Lombard 1996: 71.
13 Abaza 1988: 1–2, however, claims that 'natural conditions, such as the harsh desert climate accompanied by excessive rains and the loss of the yield, the decline of certain markets, but also the wish to escape political tyranny, the exercise of violence, feuds and rebellions, religious confessionalism, attempts at assassinations of successive *imams* seemed commonplace or simply the quest for wealth and discovery, are all reasons, which since old times have enforced migration'; see also Baldry 1984.
14 Hadhramaut comprises the fourth and fifth provinces of the People's Republic of South Yemen (roughly 112,000 sq. miles) whose capital is Sana'a. In 1979, the population was estimated at 1.9 million (Koszinowski 1983). Hadhramaut is well known for its many intellectual centres, such as the holy cities of Tarim and Saiwun. Shibam is the largest city and Wadi Hadhramaut is the most populated and agriculturally cultivated area in the region.
15 One of the four law schools of orthodox Islam founded by M. bin Idris al-Shafi'i. These schools date from the 9th century and are rites and not dissenting sects. See also Gaudefroy-Demombynes 1961: 67–68; and Makdisi 1990: chs 1 and 2.
16 Zaydism originated around the person of Zayd ibn Ali, the grandson of Ali ibn Abi Thalib, cousin of the Prophet and the fourth caliph of Islam, and is connected genealogically with the branch of Hassan and Zayn al-Abidin. Zayd struggled against the Ommayads in Damascus and was killed in 122 AH/ 740 CE. The Zaydis regard themselves as the fifth school of al-Madhhab al-Kharnis as a parallel school to the Sunni four (Renaud 1984: 57–68).
17 See also Van den Berg 1886; Bujra 1971; Serjeant 1981; Chelhod 1984; and Abaza 1988. For the last three strata Van den Berg, Bujra and Chelhod each give different and more concrete explanations. Serjeant has the most expansive detail on the Sayyid of Hadhramaut.
18 According to Abaza 'the Sayyid and Sheikhs are families or clans in which special qualities, virtues of a spiritual kind and nobility (*sharaf*) are held to reside – qualities termed by modern Arab writers *al-sultat al-ruhiyah*' op. cit.: 7.

or Du'afa, the 'poor' or 'weak' lower orders. According to traditional Arabic accounts, the ancestor of the Sayyid group in the Hadhramaut was a person called Sayyid Ahmad bin 'Isa, known as al-Muhajir, who made the 'migration', as his title indicates, southward from Mecca (Berg 1886: 34–36; Ahmad 1976: 16). To distinguish themselves from other Sayyid groups, such as in Mecca and Morocco, those living in the Hadhramaut are called al-'Alwi (plural al-'Alawiyin) after the grandchildren of Ahmad bin 'Isa (Serjeant 1981).[19]

Seven generations after Ahmad bin 'Isa, the genealogy of the Sayyid group formed branches with two sons of Muhammad, who were labelled *Sahib ar-Robat* and further divided into several clans. A list of the Sayyid clan names is presented following Van den Berg (1886) in Table 2 below.

Table 2: The names of Sayyid clans in Hadhramaut

As-Saqqaf	Abu-Numai	Al-Fad'aq
Al-Ba'aqil	Al-'Aidrus	Al-Khird
Al-Musyiyyikh	At-Taha	Al-Khunaiman
As-Sag	Al-Batumar	Al-Ba'ali
Al-Munawwar	Ali bin Syihab ad-Din[a]	Al-Gaisah
Al-Had	Al-Masyhur	Al-Bar
Az-Zahir	As-Sulaibiyyah	Al-Baraqah
Al-Mawla ad-Dawilah	Al-Moqaibil	Al-Bid
Al-MawlaKhailah	Ali bin Sahil[b]	Al-Qadri
Ali bin Yahya[c]	Al-Ba'abud[d]	Al-Baharum
Al-Hinduan	Al-Mahjub	Asy-Syatiri
Al-'Abdal-Malik	Al-Hasyim[e]	Al-Muhdar
Al-Sumait	An-Nadir	Al-Babaraik
Al-Tahir	Al-Husain al-Qarah	Al-Bahusain
Al-Haddad	Al-Bafaqih	Al-Hut
Al-Bafaraj	Ali bin Qitban	Al-Hamil
Al-Basurrah	Al-Hudaili	Al-Kaf
Al-'Aidid[f]	Al-Junaid[g]	Al-Jufri[h]
Asy-Syilli	Al-Barum	Al-Bilfaqih
Al-Muniffir	Al-Hamid	As-Serf
Asy-Syanbal	Al-Bassy-Syaiban	Al-Habsyi
Al-Musawa	Al-Baiti[i]	Al-Jamal al-Lail
Al-Ismail	Al-Maknun[j]	and others.

---

19 All of the current population of Hadhramaut, with the exception of a number of middle-class families and slaves, consider themselves to be the posterity of one Ya'rub bin Qahtan bin Hud (see Patji 1991).

Ali bin Barahim	Al-Basyumailah	
At-Tawil	Al-'Aqil bin Salim	
Al-'Attas	Asy-Syaikh Abu Bakar[k]	
Al-Haddar	Abu Futaim	
Al-Mutahhar	Al-Mudir	
Al-Marzak	Al-Mudaihij	

a. Usually called with a short name, Ali bin Syihab, ibid.
b. There are three families holding the name, ibid.
c. One branch of the family, ibid.
d. There are three families holding the name, ibid.
e. There are two families holding the name, ibid.
f. The family of Sayyid Jalaluddin al-'Aidid and to whom the Sayyid in Cikoang belong.
g. There are two families holding the name, op. cit.
h. One branch of the family is Al-Bahar, ibid.
i. There are two families holding the name, ibid.
j. There are two families holding the name, ibid.
k. The family has two branches, al-Husein and al-Hamid, ibid.
Source: Following Van den Berg 1886.

Several clans on this list no longer exist in the Hadhramaut, yet this does not mean that their descendants are not still alive. For instance, the descendants of the Bassy-Syaiban family still live in Java and those of the al-Qadri in Pontianak (Van den Berg 1886: 36; Lombard 1996: 71; Patji 1991) and, as described in this thesis, the descendants of al-'Aidid, while there are as-Shaqqaf (Assaqqaf or Assegaf) families living in Mandar, South Sulawesi.

In 1885, the Hadhramis numbered approximately 20,000 throughout Indonesia: 10,888 in Java and Madura and 9,613 in other islands (Berg 1886: 107, 109). In 1905, they numbered 29,588: 19,148 in Java and Madura and 10,440 in other regions. By 1934, between 20 and 30 per cent of all Hadhramis lived in the East Indies, East Africa and the Red Sea countries (Serjeant 1981: 24–29; Abaza 1988: 15; Roff 1964: 81) accounting for a massive pattern of outmigration.[20]

In the Indies, the Hadhramis settled along the northern coast of Java in big cities such as Batavia (Jakarta), Pekalongan, Semarang and Surabaya, as well as in Palembang in South Sumatra. The majority of them were subsistence traders, but some were fishermen and a small number were manual labourers. Many of them became extremely rich because they owned ships, property and buildings, which were very profitable (Lombard 1996: 71). Before the 20th century, Arab society seems to have founded and largely controlled the Hajj industry of the

---

20   Van den Berg 1886: 10, has argued that it is not possible to enquire about Arab 'colonies' as such before the 19th century; prior to that there were small numbers of settlers living in the most important ports of the East Indian Archipelago, often holding influential political roles on behalf of the local peoples.

Great Pilgrimage to Mecca from the Indian Archipelago (Berg 1886). In the period of 1900–1940, however, most pilgrims travelled by Dutch or British steamers and the colonial government controlled most of the process.

In addition, Arab traders (particularly the non-Sayyid, either Hadhramis or other Arabs) created the school network of al-Irshad in their settlements. The Jami'at al-Islam wal-Irshad al-Arabia (Arab Association of Islam and Guidance) was founded in Jakarta in 1913 (Noer 1973). The organisation's founders 'chafed at the deference demanded of them by those Arabs in Indonesia who claimed the status of Sayyid and sole religious scholars'. They formed al-Irshad to promote equality in social treatment and educational advancement within the Arab community. They found religious support for their emphasis on social equality in the writings of modernist Muslims and consequently turned increasingly to developing educational institutions (Noer 1973: 62).[21]

In relation to Cikoang, the advent of the Arab Sayyid is traced to the coming of Sayyid Jalaluddin al-'Aidid to the region (Pelras 1985:113). Traditional records tell that it was toward the end of the 16th century that he arrived in the archipelago, stopping first in Aceh. He then left for Banjarmasin, where it is known that his preaching was strongly tinged by Shi'ite influences. From Banjar he travelled across to Cikoang, via Gowa, where he married the daughter of a Makassar nobleman (Pelras 1985: 113; cf. Hamonic 1985: 176).[22]

According to Pelras (1985), Sayyid Jalaluddin's grandfather originally came from Iraq and resided for a while in Hadhramaut. From there he went on to Aceh. The Sayyid family living in Cikoang believe that the Sayyid Ahmad bin 'Isa mentioned above is the forebear of Sayyid Jalaluddin al-'Aidid (see Table 3 this volume). Pelras implies that Sayyid Jalaluddin was actually born in Aceh, but local Cikoang oral sources see him as coming straight from the Hadhramaut, just as they might wish to push back the time frame of events. Pelras's view is that it might be in the first years of the 17th century that Sayyid Jalaluddin came to Cikoang and founded the Sayyid community in the region (see Chapter Two).

The Hadhrami Sayyid, wherever they settle, insist on maintaining their social status through their systems of genealogy and *kafa'ah* (that there must be equality of rank between marriage partners) in marriage matches (Abaza

---

21 'Their religious leader was Syeikh Ahmad Surkati, born in the Sudan in 1872. He had taught in Mecca, where he had become impressed with the writings of the Egyptian reformer Muhammad 'Abduh. Surkati was recruited by the Indonesian Arab community and arrived in Jakarta in 1911. From 1913 until his death in 1943 he served as the spiritual leader of al-Irshad. The organization quickly established schools throughout Java and in the 1930s the Surabaya branch created a two-year course to train religious teachers.' See Noer 1973. There is no information regarding the Makassar branch of al-Irshad.
22 His wife, I-Accara Daeng Tamami, was the daughter of Gowa nobility and one of the closest relatives of the ruler of Gowa. From this marriage Sayyid Jalaluddin had three children, two sons and one daughter: Sayyid Umar, Sayyid Sahabuddin and Sayyidah Saharibonang al-'Aidid (Nurdin et al., op. cit.: 34).

1988: 15). For example, members of the al-'Aidid family, in order to prove themselves as descendants of that Sayyid clan display certificates showing their genealogical links with the al-'Aidid back to the Prophet Muhammad's family itself. All household heads retain evidential copies of the bloodline links. This certification distinguishes the Sayyid from the local people.

In order to preserve their genealogy and their identity as Arabs, the Sayyid adopt the principle of *kafa'ah*, thus arranging marriages of their children into other Sayyid families (see Chapter Three). Yet, unlike the Sayyid women, who are bound to *kafa'ah*, the men can marry women of other descent if there is no suitable Syarifah spouse in prospect. This matrimonial exchange has, in fact, added to the numbers of the Sayyid population, because the children automatically inherit the family name and Sayyid status of their father. On the other hand, it is equally said to be a 'network of assimilation' with the local people (Patji 1991). These two practices of guarding genealogy and *kafa'ah* make the Sayyid community exclusive wherever they settle and such traces are quite apparent in Cikoang, Ujung Pandang and Jakarta.

CHAPTER TWO

The *Lontara*': The Bugis-Makassar Manuscripts and their Histories

Time and place are the general parameters of history. Historiographic traditions may vary in the methods they rely upon, the evidence they accept and the conceptions of the world they seek to justify. But, all forms of historiography from the simplest of oral traditions to the most sophisticated of literary endeavours must be concerned with relating certain structured events within some framework of time and place. To be a history, a narrative must establish a chronology and a location (Fox 1979: 10).

This chapter will demonstrate the utilisation of *lontara'*, the Bugis-Makassar manuscripts and *caritana turioloa* (the 'stories of the elders') as historical sources. Both have been used by Indonesianists – Indonesian and non-Indonesian – with special reference to the history of the Islamisation of South Sulawesi in general and Cikoang in particular. In historical studies of South Sulawesi many observers have relied on the written *lontara'* as their references. This may be due to the well-documented information available in them (Cense 1951), covering such matters as length of the reigns of kings of Makassar, dates of wars among Bugis kingdoms and the process of local conversion to the world religion of Islam. It is therefore necessary to look at the evidence regarding the frequent use of *lontara'* as primary sources.

However, the aim of this chapter is not to give a historiography of the *lontara'* manuscripts.[1] Instead, my aim is to apply the *lontara'* more specifically to the study of Islam in South Sulawesi. The chapter also discusses the use of

---

1   For a more concrete elaboration of Bugis-Makassar historiography see Cense 1951: 42–60; Noorduyn 1961, 1965; Abidin 1971, 1974; and Caldwell 1988.

Cikoangese stories of the elders, the *caritana turioloa* or what Fox (1979) calls 'historical narratives' in the interpretation of the coming of Sayyid Jalaluddin al-'Aidid to Cikoang.

The Islamisation of South Sulawesi according to the *lontara'*

In this section, I shall consider popular understandings of the history of South Sulawesi based on information in the *lontara'* (see Appendix I). To begin with, let us consider the following quotation:

> The process of Islamisation in Indonesia (particularly South Sulawesi) can be reckoned into two clearly separate stages: the coming of Islam and conversion to Islam. The former is the time of trading movements in the archipelago of Indonesia and the latter consists of specific times in the history of Indonesia's ethnic groups' Islamisation. If necessary, there follows a third stage, which is the spreading of Islam by either forceful or peaceful means.[2]

Located on the southern tip of Sulawesi, Makassar seems to have been in contact with Islam since a time of rivalry between outside traders (chiefly Malays) and local merchants (Reid 1993: 132–136). Both Portuguese and Makassar sources state that by the early 16th century, Malay Muslim traders had settled in Makassar and other places on the southwest coast of Sulawesi (Noorduyn 1956). Nevertheless, historians argue that in reality it was many years before Makassar adopted Islam on any significant scale.

According to the *lontara' bilang* (Matthes 1883: 155–156) in the reign of Karaeng Tunipallangga (c. 1546–1565), a Javanese named Nakoda Bonang was residing in Gowa, and other Muslims from Makassar, Campa, Patani, Pahang, Johor and Minangkabau gained a number of privileges there. The building of a mosque[3] for the community in the Mangalekanna suburb of Makassar was granted by Tunipallangga's successor, Tunijallo (c. 1565–1590). At this time, there were also wider trading connections established with other regions of the archipelago, which Pelras (1985) named a 'Campa-Patani-Aceh-Minangkabau-Banjarmasin-Demak-Giri-Ternate network'.

---

2   My translation from the Dutch. See Noorduyn 1956: 247–266, and 1965. According to Abidin 1971: 163 'the *lontara'* which Noorduyn studied date from the eighteenth century, though some were originally composed in the seventeenth'. See also Arnold 1913.

3   The mosque, called Katangka Mosque, is still standing in the vicinity of the Gowa Royal Tombs, where Karaeng Matoaya (I Mallingkaang Daeng Nyonri Karaeng Katangka), ruler of Tallo and prime minister of Gowa and the first person believed to become Muslim in 1605, lies buried (Reid and Reid 1988: 58).

Pelras (1985: 108) has also suggested that the coming of Islam to South Sulawesi, particularly to Gowa, might be related to the legend of the 'Three Datok' (Mak. Dato' Tallua and Bug. Dato' Tellue) who were the *muballigh*, or preachers, who introduced Islam. The date of the arrival of the Three Datok, if we refer to the Kutei Chronicle, was around 1575. The legend of the Three Datok, which is similar to those of the Wali Songo, the Nine Saints of Java, is regarded as the first period of the Islamic mission in Gowa. These Three Datok, Abdul Makmur Khatib Tunggal (alias Datok ri Bandang), Khatib Sulaiman (alias Datok ri Pattimang) and Khatib Bungsu (alias Datok ri Tiro) are believed to have succeeded in converting the twin states of Gowa and Tallo' (see Appendix II).

A number of oral traditions mention that before the Three Datok arrived in Gowa they first went to Luwu' (now Palopo) (see Appendix II),[4] a Bugis kingdom in South Sulawesi, in order to convert the ruler of Luwu' – Datu' Payung Luwu' (The Umbrella of Luwu') named La Patiware Daeng Parabbung – who allegedly pronounced the *syahadat*, the Islamic profession of faith signifying conversion, on 15 or 16 Ramadhan 1013 AH (4th or 5th February 1604) and adopted the Arabic title Sultan Muhammad (Daeng Patunru 1983: 19).

The twin states of Gowa and Tallo', referred to by Dutch writers as *zusterstaten*, 'sister kingdoms', are inseparable in the history of South Sulawesi. This relationship is described in a traditional saying of the peoples of Gowa and Tallo' as *rua karaeng nase're ata*, 'two rulers but only one people' (Daeng Patunru 1983: 9). The ruler of Tallo' and also prime minister of Gowa, named Karaeng Matoaya (I Mallingkaang Daeng Manyonri Karaeng Katangka), was believed to have first embraced the Islamic faith with several members of his family on Thursday night, 9 Jumadil Awal 1014 AH (22nd September 1605) and hence after the Luwu' ruler's conversion in 1604.

As the first ruler to pronounce the *syahadat* in the Makassar region, he assumed the title Sultan Abdullah Awalul Islam. At the same time, the ruler of Gowa, who was his nephew and student, I Manga'rangi Daeng Manrabbia by name, also became a Muslim, taking the title of Sultan Alauddin. This legendary tale is explicitly expressed in the following traditional poem:[5]

Hera 1605, Hijarak Sanak 1015,
22 Satemberek, 9 Jumadelek awalak, bangngi Jumak.

---

4   Pelras (1985) states that 'when Datok Pattimang arrived in Bua, to the south of Palopo, he was welcomed by a nobleman called Tenriajeng, who was the first local Muslim there, and that is why he is known also as I Assalang, from *asal*, or origin. He had kept his conversion secret because nobody in the nobility could claim to have embraced Islam as long as the Luwu' ruler was not a Muslim himself, and that is why he was called also Tenripau, Not-to-be-mentioned.'
5   Excerpt from the *urupu sulapa' appa* or *lontara'*, *Lontara Bilang Raja Gowa dan Tallo'* (Diary of the Kings of Gowa and Tallo) 1985/1986, Dep. Dik. Bud. Bidang Penelitian dan Pengkajiang Kebudayaan Sulawesi Selatan La Galigo.

Namantama Islaam Karaenga rua sisarikbattang.

In 1605 AD[6], and the Hijri year 1015,
On 22 September, or Jumadil Awal, on Thursday evening,
The two kings and brothers embraced Islam.

Hera 1607, Hijarak Sannak 1017,
9 Nopemberek, 18 Rakjab, allo Jumak.
Nauru mamenteng jumaka ri Tallok, uru sallanta.

In 1607, and the Hijri year 1015,
On 9 November, or 18 Rajab, on Friday,
The Juma'ah prayers were first said in Tallok, (thus it was) the beginning of Islam.

The tale of the Three Datok and their mission conveys the impression that the expansion of Islam in the major part of South Sulawesi was very rapid. Within two years after the conversion of the two rulers, all the citizens of the Gowa and Tallo' kingdoms had accepted the new faith and the two kingdoms became centres of wider Islamisation in South Sulawesi. The ruler of Gowa began to convince other rulers in alliance with his kingdom throughout South Sulawesi to accept Islam. At first not all were happy with the mission. Some rejected it as unfriendly, especially the three largest Bugis kingdoms of Bone, Wajo and Soppeng (Daeng Patunru 1983: 20; Hamid 1994: 11). Their rejection angered the ruler of Gowa and he waged war on the Bugis until they accepted Islam.[7]

According to Daeng Patunru (1983), however, the king of Gowa was regarded as a good Muslim and adhered to the principle of the teaching that the expansion of Islam must be carried out by peaceful means. He did not force the Bugis rulers to accept the new faith, but because they had mounted opposition towards the influence and authority of Gowa,[8] he necessarily had to be harsh toward them in order to preserve his own power and sovereignty in South Sulawesi.[9]

On the other hand, Robinson and Paeni (1998) argue that the war was due to a treaty held by the descendants of the kings of Gowa/Makassar and those of the Bugis. The traditional agreement had stated 'if anyone deriving from either Makassar or Bugis, or others, finds a spark of goodness, the discoverer of it will

---

6   Noorduyn (1956: 15–21) argues, however, that none of the sources give exact numbers of the years in this chronicle. See the diary published by Ligtvoet, Transcriptie van he dagboek der vorsten van Gowa en Tallo met vertaling en aantekeningen, in *Tijdschrift van het Bataviaasch Genotschap* (TBG) 1880, Vol IV, which records 1603. We can now assume this to be an error, possibly misremembered by the writer of the chronicle.
7   For the Buginese, the war is regarded as the *musuk selling*, Islamic war (Hamid 1994: 11).
8   These two ethnic groups of Makassar and Bugis are culturally related, but historically have been rivals for dominance in the peninsula. Pelras 1975: 6; and Mills 1975: 217–218.
9   See Arnold 1913 for different reasons for the war.

be obliged to convince the others.' Accordingly, the Gowa kingdom had chosen Islam because it presented such a spark of goodness and needed to be shared among other kingdoms.

Before the Bugis and Makassarese nobles officially accepted Islam they had faced a choice between Islam and Christianity. They had begun to doubt the meaning of their own pre-Islamic faith and its strength as a source of worldly power. Arnold (1913: 394) describes what followed: 'Thus they determined to send, at the same time, to Malacca (which was under the control of the Portuguese) and to Aceh (an Islamic kingdom) to desire from the one, Christian priests and from the other, Islamic missionaries, resolving to embrace the religion of those missionaries who came first among them.' The Bugis and Makassarese nobilities finally accepted Islam because it was the Islamic missionaries who arrived first, while their demands for Christian priests went unanswered by the Portuguese (cf. Pelras 1985: 115).

Within seven years, all kingdoms in Sulawesi were converted to Islam. These were respectively Luwu' in 1604, the twin Gowa-Tallo' in 1605, Sidrap-Soppeng in 1609, Wajo in 1610 and Bone in 1611. Despite their forced entry into Islam, the Bugis people are in present times considered to be among pious Muslims and in possession of great religious teachers. When they settle farther afield from home they are successful in introducing Islam to local peoples and traces of their influence can be found in Maluku, Flores, Banjarmasin, Irian Jaya and other provinces of Indonesia where they have gone in order to make a better life for themselves.

Nevertheless, the process of Islamic expansion in South Sulawesi took a very long period of time, incorporating a lengthy process of 'familiarisation' (Pelras 1985: 110) characterised by a tendency to mediate Islam with traditional beliefs (In. and Ar. *adat*). There are traditions in the *lontara'* stating that for 125 years before the official acceptance of Islam, the people of South Sulawesi had been in regular contact with Muslim merchants. Pelras (1985: 110–114) has argued that the people of Makassar, and probably the Buginese with their rulers as well, had modified Islam with their traditional beliefs for a long time before they decided to embrace it fully.

The aforementioned Three Datok managed to draw parallels between the Shariah of Islam and customary *adat* of place, so that Islam was not seen as a wholly alien belief system. Islam was acceptable, because many of its ethical teachings also existed in local values. In their view, this method had to be applied because, as Noorduyn (1956: 247–266) suggests, Islam also brought with it radical implications that induced strong resistance among people who were keenly attached to their traditions and proud of their own culture. The conversion to Islam by Karaeng Matoaya, followed by his family and later by his people, could take place because the Three Datok chose to come to terms with the local traditions in the hope that their teaching and *dakwah* would in the long term make the older beliefs irrelevant.

The Three Datok insisted that the act of proclaiming conversion must be the first priority; a complete implementation of Islamic values would follow in the long term (Pelras 1985: 122). In due course members of the local nobility were appointed as officials administering Islamic observance, such as the *imam*, the leader of the ritual prayers; the *khatib* or preacher of sermons; the *bilal* or caller to *prayer*; and the *qadhi*, or legal judge. These incumbents were called Parewa Sara', 'Instruments of the Syari'at' (Pelras 1985: 122) and formed another council within the social traditions of Makassar. The only council known before the coming of Islam had been the Ade', the gathering of traditional chiefs as the guardians of the customs and practices of the community. The two councils of the Ade' and Parewa Sara' were then allocated side by side to be advisers over the kingdoms and were known collectively as Pangngadakkang in Makassarese and Pangngadereng in Buginese (Andaya 1984).

It was in this way that agreement was finally achieved between the Three Datok and the local nobility. Datuk Pattimang, for example, used teachings centred on *tauhid* (Ar. the absolute oneness of God) not strictly in Islamic terms, but by invoking Bugis beliefs about the One God, Dewata Seuwae (in Makassar, Karaeng Kaminang Kammaya), from whom the Tomanurung, claimed as founders by both Makassarese and Bugis were descended, and the Parewa Sara' who were regarded as the representatives of the One God on Earth. Andaya (1984: 36) comments:

> By becoming a member of the Muslim nobility, he would be acknowledged as sharing the God-given privilege of being superior to the rest of humankind and of being God's Shadow on Earth. How reassuring would have been the thought that on becoming Muslim nobility, he would be justified in confronting the *adat* leaders with the statement that 'to dispute with kings is improper, and to hate them is wrong', and so to confidently anticipate the blessings of God and the entire Muslim community.

To offer another example, Datok ri Bandang did not try to force the Makassar nobility immediately after they had embraced Islam to do away with traditional customs, such as bringing offerings to sacred places and the belief in *saukang*,[10] symbols found in nature, because such were regarded as the means to guarantee prosperity for the society and represented a chain between the present rulers

---

10   These were believed to contain 'magical properties that could ensure the well-being of the community. The *saukang* may have been a mango pit or a piece of wood, but most often it was a stone. The finder of the *saukang* became the temporary personification of the deity immanent in the *saukang* and the intermediary or link between the god on the one hand and the community on the other.' (Andaya 1984: 25.)

and their forebears[11] (Pelras 1985: 124). Accordingly, the Makassar nobility did not abandon the local traditions that they conceived as central to their culture, but by holding Islamic offices such as *imam, bilal, qadhi* and *khatib* their dignity and prestige became more the exalted in the eyes of society. It was also through these Islamic offices that the Makassar nobility became the central agents of Islamisation in South Sulawesi (Daeng Patunru 1983).

The role of Muslim traders as *muballigh*, or religious missionaries, is also well known in relation to the history of Indonesian Islamisation. Indeed, their coming to South Sulawesi was not just for trade, but also to introduce Islam to their local counterparts. What is more, not all the Malays coming to South Sulawesi were traders; many of them were just *muballigh* who came at the invitation of the local people.

Trading connections between Muslim Malays and the local merchants became a bridge through which the *muballigh* entered into easy contact with the local people. It was a partnership in which they could introduce the Islamic faith by friendly means. Islam secured its roots in South Sulawesi in the early 17th century, or according to the official account, 22nd September 1605 (which 'official' conversion to Islam is relatively late when compared to other regions, such as Sumatra and Java).

The distinction between the coming of Islam and 'official Islamisation' must be made, however. For instance, although the Three Datok – as Malay *muballigh* originating from Minangkabau, namely Datok ri Pattimang (alias Sulaiman Khatib Sulung) active in the Luwu' and Wajo' kingdoms; Datok ri Tiro (alias Abd ul-Jawad Khatib Bungsu) in Bulukumba; and Datok ri Bandang (alias Abd ul-Makmur Khatib Tunggal) in Gowa – had come into contact with the Bugis and Makassar aristocrats after their arrival in 1575, the conversion of the Makassarese and Buginese noblemen to Islam was only achieved in 1605 after a relationship lasting 30 years.

The mythological character of Sayyid Jalaluddin

Masyarakat di sekitar kediaman I-Bunrang memberikan perhatian penuh
atas keberadaan seseorang yang bertampang Arab
dengan wajah anggun penuh wibawa dan rendah hati.

Sampai setiap orang yang menemuinya sangat terkesan
dan menjadi terpikat terutama pada kepribadiannya yang senantiasa memancarkan

---

11 'Highland Makassarese called their pre-Islamic religion *patuntung* from a root that means 'to strive', because it was essentially about competitively manipulating spirits to increase status in this world and the next.' (Reid 1993: 138).

kata-kata 'hikmah' dan tidak lepas dari menyebut nama Allah.

The people living around I-Bunrang's residence gave their full attention
to the presence of that person of Arab appearance, he was
of elegant and authoritative mien, yet of unpretentious comportment.

So that all who met him were impressed
and drawn to him, especially to his character and the way in which he spoke
words of wisdom, never unmindful of reciting the name of Allah.
(Haji Maluddin Daeng Sikki, Cikoang, January 1997)

The verses above tell the tale well known among the Cikoangese of the first contact of Sayyid Jalaluddinal-'Aidid with the local people. The descriptions of his character and his Islamic piety show that he made a great impression in the minds of the Cikoangese from the very time of his arrival. Nowadays people still refer to him whenever they talk about religious activities. However, there is doubt about exactly when and why Sayyid Jalaluddin came to Cikoang. What actually was the character of his teachings? The only available sources are in the possession of the Cikoangese themselves, in old manuscripts and chronicles that are extremely difficult to obtain due to the sacredness in which the artefacts are regarded. They are restricted from outsiders (as the writer himself experienced) and even among the Cikoangese themselves. The only people entitled to have access to these old manuscripts are those categorised as *anrongguru* or religious specialists (see Chapter Four) and who are currently rare to find. Sayyid Maluddin Daeng Sikki al-'Aidid (Sayyid Karaeng) who is Chair of the al-'Aidid organisation of Makassar is one from whom I was able to obtain several modern transcripts of the old texts. These contain the history of the coming of Sayyid Jalaluddin, the grounds of conducting the Maudu' ceremony and other such Sayyid traditions.[12]

---

12   The transcripts that I obtained were made in 1996. Besides collecting data through a series of scheduled interviews with informants, I also received several written pieces of information given by my key informant, Sayyid H. Maluddin Daeng Sikki.

2. The *Lontara'*

Figure 1: Portrait of Sayyid Jalaluddin al-'Aidid
Source: Haji Maluddin Daeng Sikki, Cikoang, January 1997.

Every observer conducting research into the Cikoangese community must depend heavily on the information given by the *anrongguru* which has been handed down orally from generation to generation. For instance, French scholars Gilbert Hamonic (1985) and Christian Pelras (1985) as well as Indonesian observers such as Muhammad Hisyam (1983), having observed the distinctiveness of the religious life of the Cikoangese, could not avoid adopting the information of the *anrongguru*. We shall see how these stories of the elders, *caritana turioloa* .provide the special perceptions of the Cikoangese historical accounts.

In the period of South Sulawesi's early contact with Muslim Malay regions of the archipelago, it is told that Cikoangese sailing to Aceh had met two figures named Hapeleka, who had an excellent memorisation of the Qur'an and a Saeha (Syeikh). They encountered an *ulama* whose genealogy was derived from the Hadhramaut, namely Sayyid Jalaluddin al-'Aidid.[13] The Cikoangese then requested Sayyid Jalaluddin to come to Sulawesi. Muhammad Hisyam says (1985: 18) that on his voyage to Makassar, Sayyid Jalaluddin put in at Kutai, Kalimantan where he met Abdul Kadir Daeng Malliongi' or Bambanga ri Gowa, a Makassarese nobleman who had been forced to flee because of a *siri'* elopement scandal (see further Chapter Three on *siri'*). Sayyid Jalaluddin instructed Daeng Malliongi' in Islam and subsequently married his daughter, I-Accara Daeng Tamami.

Prior to his arrival in Cikoang, while in Gowa, Sayyid Jalaluddin al-'Aidid was reported to have been appointed by the ruler of Gowa, Abd. Kadir Karaenta ri Bura'ne as his adviser, particularly in matters of military tactics and religious studies (Ar. *din ul-Islam*). It is Sayyid Jalaluddin's holding of this historic strategic rank, along with their socially ascribed status which leads the Sayyid of Cikoang to consider themselves to be of higher moral and religious worthiness than the Makassar nobility.

Though Sayyid Jalaluddin al-'Aidid had no problems with the local people in Gowa he met with some sort of opposition from the king. He moved to Cikoang, where he converted the still pagan nobility and population. But according to Hamonic (1985) and Cikoang sources, the hostility between Sayyid Jalaluddin and the ruler was not the cause for his moving. Rather, Sayyid Jalaluddin saw that Islam had become the major faith of Gowan society and there were already in circulation teachings of a number of influential scholars, such as the Acehnese

---

13 According to Cikoang sources, Sayyid Jalaluddin was a son of Sayyid Muhammad Wahid of Aceh and one Syarifah Halisyah. The latter's father, Sayyid 'Alawiyah Jala ul-Alam was himself a son of one Sayyid Muhajirun al-Basrah. Exiled from Basrah, he had fled Iraq at the beginning of the 16th century because of political troubles, possibly connected to the wars between the Ottoman empire and the kingdom of Iran, which erupted in 1514 (see Pelras 1985).

Hamzah Fansuri and Nuruddin ar-Raniri, men of different descent (Persian and Hadhrami Arab respectively), culture and competing Sufi *tarekats*, which had been embraced by the local people.

There are other versions of the story of this matter in Cikoang traditions; for instance, that Sayyid Jalaluddin met the opposition of the ruler of Gowa because he refused to tell of his earlier life – probably the fact of his marriage to the daughter of the exiled Daeng Malliongi'. The chief version, more logical to the Sayyid and the one used in this study, is that Sayyid Jalaluddin left Gowa because he did not want to see the unity of Muslims disturbed by his presence. It should be noted that the law school of Gowa had been established as the Madzab Syafi'i of Sunni Islam, whereas Sayyid Jalaluddin was of the Shi'i Zaydi school of Yemen which emphasised adherence to its own mystical brotherhood, the Tarekat Bahr ul-Nur (Ar. the Mystical Way of the Sea of Light). It is possible that he was unwilling to risk introducing a rival discipline into Gowa. This historical event took place in 1032 AH/1632 CE, according to the manuscript book written by Hapeleka called *Bayanul Bayan* (see further Hisyam 1985; 17–20).

Following suggestions by the ruler of Gowa, Sultan Alauddin and Karaeng Matoaya (I Mallingkaang Daeng Nyonri Karaeng Katangka), Sayyid Jalaluddin then decided to move and to take all of his family with him to Cikoang. His arrival there is still commemorated every year on Maudu', the festival of the birth of the Prophet (see further Chapter Five).

The spread of the teachings of Sayyid Jalaluddin and his followers

The status of the Sayyid is significant within the community of Cikoang because their presence is always associated with the excellence of the Prophet Muhammad as founder of the Muslim community. The way the Sayyid perpetuate their traditional status is based on the teachings historically brought by Sayyid Jalaluddin al-'Aidid as a descendant of the Prophet and the founder of that Sayyid community (Hisyam 1985).

Hamonic (1985) tells us that during his stay in Cikoang, Sayyid Jalaluddin developed a lifestyle which encouraged believers to put aside, without completely abandoning, the things of this world. He based his life on the Shariah and its sources, the Qur'an and Hadith, and on *fiqh*, or jurisprudential practices, in conjunction with his own Tarekat Bahr ul-Nur, which is focused on the quest for *hakikah*, or the reality of God, and *ma'rifatullah*, gnosis, or an intuitive knowledge of spiritual truths. In addition to these doctrines, what

Sayyid Jalaluddin emphasised most was the commemoration of Maudu' or the Maulid festival and the right methods of conducting it (discussed in detail in Chapter Five).

As the teaching of the Tarekat Bahr ul-Nur flourished, the followers of Sayyid Jalaluddin increased in number. When he thought his religious duties had finished in Cikoang, he travelled via Selayar and Buton to Sumbawa, where he died and was buried. In modern Cikoang, the Sayyid always bear in mind that the mystical order of Bahr ul-Nur is the product of the Madhhab Ahl ul-Bait – literally, the 'Way of the Household of the Prophet' (Hisyam 1985: 26) (see my further discussion in Chapter Four).

The tomb of Sayyid Jalaluddin is not located in Cikoang. Only the tomb of his second son, Sayyid Sahabuddin al-'Aidid can be found in the cemetery, Jera' Paletteka. This cemetery has traditionally been accessible only to the members of the Sayyid families. It is now regarded as a sacred site and has become popular for visitors seeking good fortune. According to Cikoang sources, Sayyid Jalaluddin died in Sumbawa, West Nusa Tenggara and was buried there. The reason why the Cikoangese did not take the body back to Cikoang for burial is that, according to my informant, the descendants of Sayyid Jalaluddin living in Sumbawa did not agree to its removal.

Sayyid Jalaluddin's second son, Sayyid Sahabuddin, settled in Cikoang, married and continued the teachings of his father. According to one Cikoang source, descendants of Sayyid Jalaluddin al-'Aidid spread out as far as Selayar, Buton, Luwu', Mandar, South Kalimantan and Jakarta (Kelurahan Penjaringan) where they are still said to be found. Moreover, with their descent maintained by strict endogamy, later generations were able to found a distinctive community around Organisasi Al-'Aidid Makassar (the Makassar Al-'Aidid Organisation). In 1905, thanks to the actions of a local Sayyid hero by the name of Bahauddin, the traditional government of Cikoang collapsed and power was taken over by the Sayyid (Hamonic 1985). Since then, the Sayyid community has dominated the appointment of the village heads of Cikoang. Such is some of the evidence of the effect of the spread of Sayyid Jalaluddin's teachings.

Hisyam (1985) observes that the election of top officials in the Cikoangese administration is rather complicated, particularly at the level of village head, due to the attitudes of the Sayyid. If the appointed village head is not from among the Sayyid, the Sayyid community will only reluctantly agree to decisions taken by him. Thus, according to Hisyam's findings, in order to better rule the Sayyid community in particular and the Cikoangese in general, the head of Mangarabombang District (an authority above Cikoang village) prefers to welcome a candidate of Sayyid origin in the election of village heads. On this point, Daeng Sila (a Sayyid Daeng) told me: 'in Punaga (another hamlet near

Cikoang village), the village head has always come from the Sayyid family, ever since the Sayyid settled in the region. The reason is because it is easy to get official approval to celebrate the Maudu' festival if the village head is a Sayyid.' It can be well understood that the appointment of village head in Cikoang is a major concern of the Cikoangese because of its impact on the maintenance of the Sayyid traditions.

To conclude: the *lontara'*, to a certain extent, provide us with adequate information about the coming of Islam to Cikoang. Although they tell us little about what really brought about the arrival of Sayyid Jalaluddin, we are at least better informed about when exactly he came to Cikoang. It was the first time Islam took root in the region, during the first years of the 17th century. In addition, the *caritana turioloa*, for the most part, not only inform us of the number of people who continued the tradition of Sayyid Jalaluddin's religious teachings, but also the details of those teachings. The complete body of the teachings will be discussed in the second part of this study.

CHAPTER THREE

Origin, Class Status and Socio-cultural Integration in Cikoang

I-bara'na cincing bulaeng,
Sayyika antu singkammai paramatanna,
Karaenga sedeng singkammai bulaenna.
Paramataya ammempoi irateanna bulaenga, tiai sibale'na.
Paramataya segang bulaenga singkamma ga'gaana,
tapi paramatayya antu kajjalangngangi.[1]

Take the example of a ring, wherein
The Sayyid is likened to the diamond,
The Karaeng to the circle of gold about,
The diamond sits atop the ring, never the other way 'round.
Both diamond and gold are equally precious,
Yet the diamond ever more costly than the gold.

In the preceding chapter we considered the stories of the coming of Sayyid Jalaluddin al'Aidid to Cikoang in the context of the advent of Islam in South Sulawesi, and of the Sayyid's socio-religious integration with the local people of Makassar. This chapter discusses the impact Sayyid Jalaluddin and his descendants made on the social structure of Cikoang. Of essential concern is the extent to which the Sayyid and Makassar social institutions have developed hand in hand throughout history. Thus I shall consider the Sayyid community as

---

1   The Indonesian version is as follows:
    Ibarat sebuah cincin permata, Sayyid itulah intan permatanya, sedangkan Karaeng sebagai emasnya. Intan selalu diatas emas dan bukan sebaliknya. Keduanya sama-sama bernilai, tapi intan selalu lebih bernilai atau berharga ketimbang emas (from taped interview with a Sayyid Karaeng).

culturally Makassarese, in most respects like other Makassar societies, without ignoring the notion of distinctive Sayyid characteristics such as titles, marriage systems and religious festivities.

The saying quoted above is often mentioned by the Sayyid to distinguish their present social position from that of the Karaeng, the Makassarese nobility. According to my Sayyid informants, the Sayyid are traditionally associated with spiritual matters – they are religious specialists and heads of ritual practice, whereas the Karaeng are historically related to secular matters as chiefs and heads of *adat* communities. Any union of the two is said to be a set of reconciliations between the religious and secular realms.

These two ascribed statuses are significant for the Cikoangese in relation to contemporary social stratification in Cikoang. The Sayyid status is said to have come into being once Sayyid Jalaluddin, together with his family, established domicile in the region, whereas the Karaeng are believed to have been present long before the coming of Sayyid Jalaluddin. Thus it is useful to identify the very beginning, or what Lewis (1996: 166) termed 'origins', of the Cikoangese people underpinning the social hierarchy as it is today. In so doing, we should not ignore notions of ancestry, place and alliance in defining individuals and social groups in Cikoang.

However, as Fox and Sather declare (1996: 5), access to origin or pedigree involves various ways of ascertainment: dreaming, contact with spirits, the recitation of formulaic wisdom, the witness of the elders or the presentation of sacred objects as proof of connections to the past; each of these means enables the presentation of information of the past.[2] As regards origins in Cikoang, the easiest access to these is the witness of the elders or what the Cikoangese call *caritana turioloa*, the 'stories of the elders'.

In this chapter I will first provide a general understanding of the social hierarchy in Cikoang. I will then discuss the Sayyid marriage system, called *kafa'ah*, which becomes the primary basis of their kinship system.

---

2   Notions of origin may vary from one society to another but are generally cited in terms of 'common metaphors based on recognizable cognate expressions'. For Fox and Sather (1996) this is a distinctive Austronesian characteristic.

Origins: Notions of ancestry and social rank

Before the arrival of Sayyid Jalaluddin and his family, the system of social subdivisions in Cikoang was similar to those of other Makassar societies. There were three major ranks: Karaeng, the nobles or chiefs; Tumaradeka, free people or commoners; and Ata, or slaves (Hisyam 1985: 126).

According to Makassar traditions, individuals regarded as Karaeng were principally limited to the children of Sombaya ri Gowa, rulers of the kingdom of Gowa called Anakkaraeng. They were distinguished by their 'white blood' inherited through the Tumanurung (*tu* meaning 'person' and *manurung* 'to descend') thus 'those who descended (from the sky)', which both the Makassarese and the Bugis claim as their founders, were the first rulers of South Sulawesi.

A traditional myth found in the *lontara'* manuscripts similarly states that the Tumanurung married the leading representative of the Makassarese people, one Karaeng Bajo. This union created the first sophisticated polity in South Sulawesi, the kingdom of Gowa. The descendants of this couple were said to be the Anakkaraeng, who held the right to rule the kingdom and inherited the 'white blood' of the Tumanurung, in distinction from the 'red blood' of the commoners (cf. Bulbeck 1992: 40). According to Bulbeck (1992: 41) 'the aristocrats were ranked by the degree to which their white blood, as traced through both parents, remained undiluted by the red blood of commoners; access to titles depended on nobility of birth. That is, status was ascribed.'[3] (See further Appendix IV.)

The Cikoangese nobles, however, were derived from what Bulbeck (1996) termed 'lesser rajas or petty royalty' compared to 'greater rajas' (e.g. the Gowa rulers) belonging to 'historical successions', that is, rulers of the Laikang kingdom (Kamaruddin et al., 1985: 169; Andaya 1984: 128, 137; cf. Bulbeck 1996). Yet the aristocrats of this kingdom and other lesser kings are also considered to be Karaeng and similar to the Anakkaraeng.

According to the *caritana turioloa*, it was Sayyid Sirajuddin, a grandson of Sayyid Jalaluddin, who first married a female aristocrat named Ranjabila Daeng Tiknok, a Laikang noblewoman (see Table 3). This is said to be the beginning of reconciliation between the Sayyid and Karaeng in Cikoang. As pioneers of Islamisation in Cikoang, the descendants of Sayyid Jalaluddin were readily welcomed by the local people, including the nobles. Their religious legitimacy

---

3   In the 15th and 16th centuries only 'pure' descendants reserved the right to rule a kingdom (Friedericy 1933; Mukhlis 1975; Acciaioli 1989; Bulbeck 1992: 41). Nonetheless, among the Makassarese a patrilateral bias obviously existed apart from the essentially bilateral manner of ascribing status (Röttger-Rössler 1989: 42–43; Mukhlis 1975: 37–38; cf. Bulbeck 1992: 281).

allowed them to claim themselves as having higher moral worthiness, which in turn led to opportunities for them to marry high-born local women. The issue of such unions for generations have formed the population of Sayyid Karaeng within the social hierarchy of Cikoang.

As a result, in modern Cikoang, as Hisyam (1985) has observed, almost all aristocrats have Sayyid blood. Due to the frequent practice of intermarriage between the Sayyid and both local noble women and those of a lower stratum, their descendants are eligible to bring together Sayyid and Karaeng descent. At present these comprise a large proportion of the Sayyid population, as Sayyid Karaeng and Sayyid Daeng. According to Achmad (1995), and my own experience in the field, a number of aristocrats are also found among the Jawi who have no Sayyid blood – but this number is relatively small. As well, among members of the Sayyid, there are those who practise a strictly endogamous marriage system of unions between a Sayyid and a Syarifah, which produces descendants called Sayyid Tuan (see further below).

Regarding the origins of the kinship system in Cikoang as a whole, there is a mythical tale recounting the first contact of Sayyid Jalaluddin with I-Danda and I-Bunrang, two famous warriors of the kingdom of Laikang. According to the *caritana turioloa*, the current patterns of the Cikoangese kinship relationship are also based on this myth. H. Maluddin Daeng Sikki narrated it to me as follows:

1. *I-Danda dan I-Bunranglah yang memanggil Sayyid Jalaluddin untuk menyebarkan Islam di Cikoang. Kedua orang itulah yang pertama-tama menjadi murid-murid Sayyid Jalaluddin.*

   It was I-Danda and I-Bunrang who invited Sayyid Jalaluddin to spread Islam in Cikoang. It was also these two men who became the first students of Sayyid Jalaluddin.

2. *Sebelum Sayyid Jalaluddin bersedia menjadi guru mereka, beliau ingin menguji sampai sejauh mana kesetiaan kedua orang tersebut kepada beliau.*

   Before Sayyid Jalaluddin would accept them to become his students, he wished to test the extent of their loyalty towards him.

3. *Cara beliau adalah dengan meminta istri-istri kedua orang tersebut untuk tinggal dirumah Sayyid Jalaluddin barang semalam.*

   How Sayyid Jalaluddin did this was to ask the wives of the two men to spend the night in his house.

4. *Mendengar permintaan tersebut, I-Bunrang, orang pertama yang dimintai oleh Sayyid Jalaluddin, langsung marah. Dan sambil mengeluarkan parang dari sarungnya dia berkata, 'saya lebih baik mati daripada menyerahkan istri saya kepada tuan'.*

Upon hearing this request, I-Bunrang, who was the first person asked, became angry, drew his sword and said, 'Better I die than give my wife to you'.

5. *Mendengar itu, Sayyid Jalaluddin mengurungkan niatnya. Beliau lalu menanyai I-Danda. Dengan berat hati I-Danda berkata, 'kalau memang hal itu betul-betul tuan inginkan, saya tidak berkeberatan atas permintaan tersebut'.*

    Upon hearing this, Sayyid Jalaluddin cancelled his intent. He then repeated his request to I-Danda. Reluctantly, I-Danda said, 'If this is truly your request, sir I cannot demur'.

6. *Lalu pulanglah I-Danda menemui istrinya dan memberitahukan segalanya. Karena ingin juga menunjukkan kesetiaan kepada suaminya, istri I-Dandapun menyetujuinya dan berdandanlah dia secantik-cantiknya kemudian berangkat ke rumah Sayyid Jalaluddin, untuk tinggal bersamanya selama satu malam.*

    I-Danda went home straightaway and informed his wife. Wanting to show her loyalty to her husband, she agreed. She attired herself at her most beautiful and went to stay in Sayyid Jalaluddin's house all night long.

7. *Keesekon harinya, Sayyid Jalaluddin mengizinkan istri I-Danda untuk kembali menemui suaminya dan menceritakan seluruh kejadian yang terjadi malam itu.*

    The next day, Sayyid Jalaluddin bade I-Danda's wife to return home and to tell her husband all that had taken place that night.

8. *I-Danda yang sedih dan sudah tidak sabar menanti istrinya kembali, kaget bercampur gembira setelah mendengar cerita istrinya bahwa selama semalam itu dia cuma diajarkan cara berwudhu' dan bersembayang oleh Sayyid Jalaluddin.*

    I-Danda, sadly and impatiently awaiting his wife's return, was surprised and overjoyed when he heard her tell that Sayyid Jalaluddin had simply taught her how to perform the prescribed ablutions and prayers.

9. *Kemudian I-Danda bertanya, apakah wudhu' dan sembayang itu? Istrinya menjawab, 'itulah Dienul Islam (Agama Islam)'.*

    I-Danda then asked to know what making ritual ablutions and Islamic ritual prayers were. His wife answered, 'They are *Dienul Islam*, (the religion of Islam)'.

10. *Setelah mendengar cerita tersebut, bersegeralah I-Bunrang dan I-Danda menemui Sayyid Jalaluddin. Sesampai disana, berpesanlah Sayyid Jalaluddin kepada kedua orang tersebut:*

    'saya menganggap kamu I-Bunrang sebagai sampopinruang (sepupu dua kali) saya, karena kamu adalah seorang pemberani. Anak cucumu boleh menikah dengan anak cucu saya. Sedangkan kamu I-Danda saya anggap sebagai saudara kandung. Anak cucumu haram hukumnya kawin dengan anak cucuku sampai akhir zaman.'

After hearing this account, I-Danda and I-Bunrang went to see Sayyid Jalaluddin. He then addressed the two men as follows:

> You I-Bunrang, I regard you as my second cousin because of your bravery. Descendants of yours and mine are allowed to intermarry. And I regard you, I-Danda as my own brother (because of your loyalty). Henceforth for all time, descendants of yours and mine are forbidden to intermarry.

Thus the descendants of I-Danda and Sayyid Jalaluddin are traditionally forbidden to marry one another, whereas the descendants of I-Bunrang can marry any of Sayyid Jalaluddin's and I-Danda's line. In reality, however, many cases of intermarriage between the descendants of Sayyid Jalaluddin and I-Danda are found. The Sayyid community is less worried about the violation of this mythical prohibition since its authenticity varies from one Sayyid to another. One Sayyid told me, 'there is no such tracing of descent through an oath, since a child can only inherit the status of Sayyid so long as his or her father is a Sayyid'.

However, as Hisyam (1985) and I myself observed, a number of people claim descent from the lines of both I-Danda and I-Bunrang and consider themselves to have familial ties with Sayyid Jalaluddin. For example, the Cikoangese living in Jalan Irian in the north of Ujung Pandang city conceive of themselves as the descendants of I-Bunrang, while retaining the right to be involved in the Maudu' or Maulid festival in Cikoang, as do other descendants of Sayyid Jalaluddin.

In their social interaction, descendants derived either from Sayyid Jalaluddin or the I-Bunrang or I-Danda lines maintain simultaneously the existence of the myth as it has been represented by their elders, reflecting a close original association between them and Kampong Cikoang. Nowadays the affiliation of all three groups represents the original inhabitants of Kampong Cikoang and are known collectively as the Cikoangese. In everyday life, however, the descendants of both I-Danda and I-Bunrang are called *keturunan I-Danda dan I-Bunrang* (the offspring of I-Danda and I-Bunrang) and are not able to use the title of Sayyid. This mode of reference distinguishes them genealogically from those of Sayyid Jalaluddin's line.

In relation to the social hierarchy of Cikoang there exist two main clusters: the Sayyid and the Jawi, each with its subdivisions. The Sayyid consist of three categories, namely:

1) Sayyid Karaeng, literally children of a Sayyid father and a Karaeng mother. This rank is socially seen as a perfect stratum, because it reconciles Sayyid (in terms of religious legitimacy) on the one hand and Karaeng (in terms of secular legitimacy) on the other. The Sayyid Karaeng form the majority of Cikoangese nobles, rulers and *anrongguru*, the religious teachers or specialists.

In principle, the Sayyid Karaeng are those who can trace their origins on both their Sayyid father's and noble mother's sides. This stratum, according to my informants, is said to have come into existence from the marriage between Sayyid Sirajuddin, the grandson of Sayyid Jalaluddin al-'Aidid, and Ranjabilla Daeng Tiknok, the daughter of a Laikang nobleman, which took place in 1729. The descendants of this union are considered to have both Sayyid and the Makassar aristocratic blood. Thus, again, status is ascribed. With such genealogical links, they are categorised and called both Sayyid and Karaeng.

Syarifah Karaeng, however, may not marry Anakkaraeng, since these are of a lower stratum, whereas the Sayyid Karaeng can marry either Syarifah or women of Anakkaraeng status. The aristocratic lines are not limited to the Laikang nobility as the cradle of the Cikoang aristocracy; they may hail from any other nobility in South Sulawesi, such as, for example, from the Bugis.

2) Sayyid Tuan. These are the pure Sayyid, the children of marriages between the Sayyid and the Syarifah and are often called Anak Tiknok ('ripe' or 'proper', thus 'proper children'). This line first began when Sayyid Sahabuddin, the second son of Sayyid Jalaluddin, married Syarifah Zaenab Assegaf, the daughter of Sayyid Syafiuddin Assegaf, in 1079 AH/1670 CE. Marriageable Syarifah are not limited to the al-'Aidid clan; they can be from any other Hadhrami Sayyid group, as here, the Assegaf.

Sayyid Tuan children take the family name of their father and not of their mother; for example, if as above the father is a Sayyid of the al-'Aidid clan and a mother is of the Assegaf clan, the children will be Sayyid or Syarifah of the al-'Aidid clan. Individuals of this group are involved in a close, or patrilateral parallel cousin marriage system, which is said to be the best arrangement. In reality, the Sayyid in Cikoang tend to find their children's future partners among their brothers' children. Thus men of the Sayyid Tuan stratum marry a woman of equal descent status to them, or marry a woman of lower descent, whereas Syarifah Tuan may marry men derived from either the same status (Sayyid Tuan) or above them (Sayyid Karaeng) only.

3) Sayyid Daeng are children born of a Sayyid father and a mother from the Tumaradeka, the 'free people', or an even lower order. It is said that individuals of this stratum are descendants of Sayyid Umar al-'Aidid, the eldest son of Sayyid Jalaluddin, who married I Dandang Daeng Rimang, the daughter of an *adat* community head in Cikoang, in 1062 AH. Preferably, individuals of this stratum marry someone of equal descent to themselves. Similar to women of the Sayyid Tuan, however, the women have the right to marry only above themselves, that is, into the Sayyid Karaeng and the Sayyid Tuan.

To summarise: the Sayyid derived from any group within the Sayyid social hierarchy principally marry women of the same (or lower) descent to themselves (Syarifah or non-Syarifah), whereas the Syarifah marry men of the same or higher descent to themselves; they are strictly limited to men of Sayyid descent (see Diagram 1).

Diagram 1: The transmission of Sayyid Descent

(I)

Male	Female	Male/Female Children
	Karaeng	= Sayyid/Syarifah Karaeng
Sayyid	Syarifah	= Sayyid/Syarifah Tuan
	Tumaradeka	= Sayyid/Syarifah Daeng

NB: The Sayyid and the Syarifah can be derived from any Sayyid clan, as listed in below, but the children will take the descent status and the family name of their father.

(II)

Male	Female	Male/Female Children
Sayyid Karaeng	Syarifah	= Sayyid/Syarifah Karaeng
	Female Karaeng	
	Syarifah Tuan	
	Syarifah Daeng	
	Female Daeng	
	Other Females	
Sayyid Tuan	Syarifah Tuan	= Sayyid/Syarifah Tuan
	Syarifah Daeng	
	Female Daeng	
	Other Females	
Sayyid Daeng	Syarifah Daeng	= Sayyid/Syarifah Daeng
	Female Daeng	
	Other Females	

NB: The Sayyid marry one of equal (or below) descent to themselves, whereas the Syarifah marry one of equal (or above) descent to themselves.

Table 3: The genealogy of Sayyid Jalaluddin al-'Aidid

(I)		(II)	
1.	Nabi Muhammad Saw	1.	Nabi Muhammad Saw
2.	Fatimah az-Zahra	2.	Fatimah az-Zahra
3.	Sayyid Amir al-Mu'minin Imam al-Husein	3.	Sayyid Amir al-Mu'minin Imam al-Husein
4.	Sayyid Ali Zainal Abidin	4.	Sayyid Ali Zainal Abidin
5.	Sayyid Muhammad Baqir	5.	Sayyid Muhammad Baqir
6.	Sayyid Ja'far as-Shadiq	6.	Sayyid Ja'far as-Shadiq
7.	Sayyid Ali al-Uraidi	7.	Sayyid Ali al-Uraidi
8.	Sayyid Muhammad an-Naqib	8.	Sayyid Muhammad an-Naqib
9.	Sayyid Isa Ahmad al-Muhajir	9.	Sayyid Isa Ahmad al-Muhajir
10.	Sayyid Ahmad al-Muhajir	10.	Sayyid Ahmad al-Muhajir
11.	Sayyid Abdullah (Ubaydillah)	11.	Sayyid Abdullah (Ubaydillah)
12.	Sayyid Alwi	12.	Sayyid Alwi
13.	Sayyid Muhammad	13.	Sayyid Muhammad
14.	Sayyid Alwi	14.	Sayyid Alwi
15.	Sayyid Ali Khala' Ghasam	15.	Sayyid Ali Khala' Ghasam
16.	Sayyid Muhammad Shahib Marbad	16.	Sayyid Muhammad Shahib Marbad
17.	Sayyid Alwi	17.	Sayyid Alwi
18.	Sayyid Faqih Abdurrahman	18.	Sayyid Faqih Abdurrahman
19.	Sayyid Faqih Ahmad	19.	Sayyid Faqih Ahmad
20.	Sayyid Abdullah	20.	Sayyid Abdullah
21.	Sayyid Muhammad	21.	Sayyid Muhammad
22.	**Sayyid Ali al-Huthoh**	**22.**	**Sayyid Ali al-Huthoh**
23.	Sayyid Abdullah al-'Aidid	23.	Sayyid Muhammad Maula al-'Aidid
24.	Sayyid Umar al-'Aidid	24.	Sayyid Ali al-'Aidid
25.	Sayyid Ali al-'Aidid	25.	Sayyid Abdullah al-'Aidid
26.	Sayyid Muhammad al-'Aidid	26.	Sayyid Abdurrahman al-'Aidid
27.	Sayyid Abu Bakar al-'Aidid		
28.	Sayyid Muhammad Wahid al-'Aidid		
29.	**Sayyid Jalaluddin al-'Aidid**		

Note: The Cikoangese descendants of al-'Aidid, either living in Cikoang or in Jakarta, follow the first column, whereas the second column is popular among the non-Cikoangese descendants of al-'Aidid residing in Jakarta. According to Tuan Hasan Syachran (a Cikoangese descendant of al-'Aidid in Jakarta), the difference between the two columns arises only after Sayyid Ali al-Huthoh (see number 22). Column II shows that Sayyid Muhammad Maula al-'Aidid (see number 23) has three children: Sayyid Ali al-'Aidid, Sayyid Abdullah al-'Aidid and Sayyid Abdurrahman al-'Aidid. The Cikoangese descendants of Al-'Aidid claim descent from Sayyid Abdullah al-'Aidid, whereas the Jakarta descendants of Al-'Aidid claim descent from Sayyid Abdurrahman al-'Aidid.

Maudu': A Way of Union with God

Diagram 2: Genealogy of H. Maluddin Daeng Sikki (a Sayyid Karaeng)

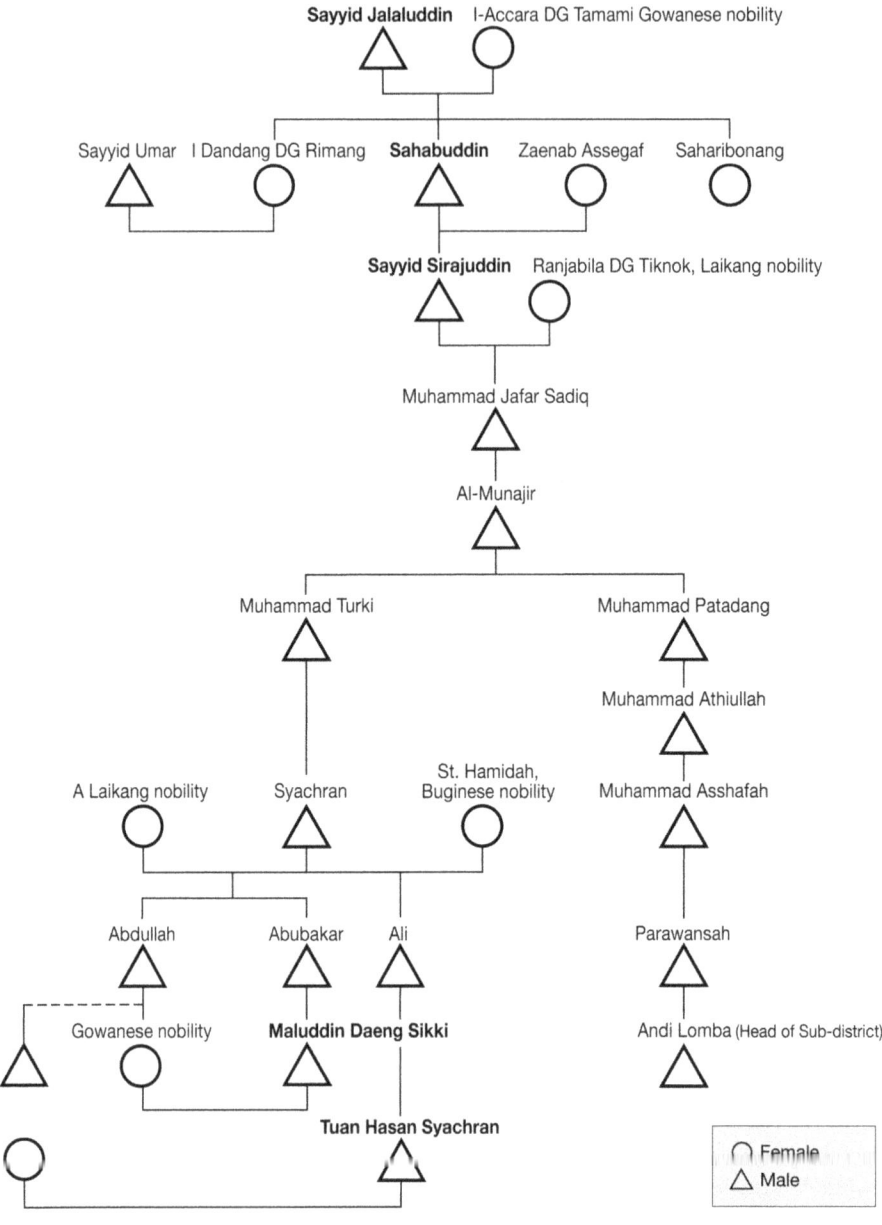

Source: Tuan Hasan Syachran al-'Aidid (a Sayyid Tuan).

The second group in the social hierarchy of Cikoang is the Jawi, or the non-Sayyid, consisting of two clusters:

1. Jawi Karaeng, the children of Karaeng, the nobility of the Laikang kingdom whose descent line remains undiluted by Sayyid blood.

2. Jawi Tumaradeka, consisting of two earlier categories, Tusamarak, or commoners, and Ata, or slaves. In present times the Tumaradeka, 'free people' have two sub-clusters:

    a. Tubajik, or 'distinguished' people who can point to peripheral family ties with the Anakkaraeng. These claim descent from the households of the Anakkaraeng because their parents or forebears have married Karaeng. Their aristocratic blood is categorised as 'indistinct' or 'half aristocratic' due to such intermarriage.

    b. Tusamarak (In. *orang kebanyakan*). These are individuals with no blood descent from the aristocracy.

In practice, the Tumaradeka and its divisions are usually identifiable by an *areng paddaengang*, or 'second name'. This is principally the highest title which a Tumaradeka, and especially a Tubajik, can attain and is granted at an early age (see Bulbeck 1992: 41). The Ata in Cikoang can be classed as Ata Sossorang, 'hereditary slaves', or children of former Ata. The majority of this group depend for their subsistence on agriculture and ship- and salt-making concerns usually owned by Sayyid Karaeng. Yet this dependency is restricted at present only within economic terms (see Appendix V). The marriage policies of these two divisions of the Jawi dictates that the men marry below themselves while the women marry above themselves.

Naming system and indications of social rank

Within their social interaction, the Anakkaraeng and the Tubajik carry an *areng pakkaraengang*, the title of Karaeng. This distinctively aristocratic title can be translated as 'chief', with 'Bugis equivalents included the Arung and Datu titles' (Bulbeck 1992). They also carry an *areng paddaengang*, the title of Daeng, or the second name, which is put after the *areng kale*, the personal or first name: e.g. Karaeng Hamid Daeng Tojeng (Mukhlis 1975 and Röttger-Rössler 1989: 45–46; cf. Bulbeck 1992) where Hamid is the given name and Daeng Tojeng the *areng paddaengang*. The *areng paddaengang* is applied at an early age, usually when an infant is first given a name. Only the Tusamarak possess an *areng paddaengang* after their given name, such as Burhan Daeng Bella, which is bestowed at an adult age or after marriage. As for the Ata, they merely have a personal or given name with no recognisable title.

According to Bulbeck (1996) the Makassar aristocratic titles (the Karaeng titles) were usually derived from the names of places where the aristocrats held authority, such as with one Makassar nobleman named Sultan Abdullah, whose full name was Palakkaya I Malingkaeng I Daeng Manyonri Karaeng Matoaya Karaeng Kanjilo Karaeng Segeri Sultan Abdullah Awalul Islam Tumenanga ri Agama Tumenanga ri Bonto Biraeng. He was the Karaeng, or chief, of three regions: Matoaya, Kanjilo and Segeri.

In regard to the Sayyid community, the Sayyid Karaeng are those who bear the titles of Karaeng and Daeng, similar to the Anakkaraeng and Tubajik titles, such as Karaeng Abdullah Daeng Lino al-'Aidid. They have their Sayyid clan appended as well, such as Karaeng Abdullah Daeng Lino al-'Aidid. The Sayyid Tuan are identified by this title at the beginning of their name and also use the Daeng title, such as in Tuan Ridwan Daeng Radja al-'Aidid.[4] While the Sayyid Daeng are parallel to the Tusamarak, they alone obtain the Daeng title, for example Sirajuddin Daeng Sila al-'Aidid. It thus appears that names of all status levels of the Sayyid employ the Daeng and al-'Aidid appellations.

Daeng Patunru (1983: 139) maintains that these divisions of social rank, including the naming system, dominate the culture, economy and religion of the Makassarese. Hamid (1994: 30), however, argues that the determination of social strata based on blood is no longer considered the only criterion, rather that Makassar social stratifications are currently based on four criteria: a) social rank and early blood descent; b) authority and its function in society; c) academic degrees and knowledge; and d) office and economic capacity or wealth. My findings agree. At the present time, even if a person cannot claim bloodline with the Anakkaraeng or the Tubajik, that person can also be called Karaeng. Such categories as wealth, strategic positions in the bureaucracy, the academic title of PhD, or even the title of Haji as a pilgrim returned from Mecca, can guarantee that a person is called Karaeng. Thus today aristocratic titles are unanimously considered to be honorary and can therefore be attached to a person of any social stratum, depending on the person's capacities in society. In spite of this, individuals of the Anakkaraeng and the Tubajik class are still regarded as more honourable, because they are in fact also among the rich, generally possessing tens of hectares of land inherited from their parents. They are the more 'honourable' with their genuine descent and wealth.

---

4   There are two different perceptions about the origins of this title of Tuan, as was argued by my informants; for example, Tuan Hasan, living in Jakarta explained that 'the term Tuan was merely an honorary title indicating someone who was a respected figure in his society'. He cited the title being given to Dutch officials in the colonial period, who mostly occupied positions in the bureaucracy. He speculated that the term Tuan could have been introduced by the Dutch. Another Sayyid Tuan told me that it was derived from Aceh, since this was the region where Sayyid Jalaluddin first stayed in the archipelago after his arrival from the Hadhramaut. The Sayyid living in Aceh use the Acehnese title Tengku, from which Tuan might have been derived.

Similarly, all levels within the Makassar social hierarchy are now entitled to obtain the Daeng title, which is then regarded as a parameter of being a Makassarese. Some Bugis also use this title, such as is done in Bone. Yet unlike the Anakkaraeng and the Tubajik, the Daeng title will only be given when a Makassarese reaches adulthood or marries.[5]

The same situation obtains in Cikoang, where in their social interaction all status levels of the Sayyid social hierarchy are called Karaeng, with no personal name attached. During my fieldwork I often heard people calling the Sayyid Karaeng, without mentioning their name: *'Iyye Karaeng'* – meaning 'Yes, Karaeng', a respectful reply when asked something by the Sayyid. So the divisions of the Sayyid are difficult to identify in daily life, except, as I noticed, when their names are fully written out or cited for personal inquiry or to appear on letters of invitation to weddings.

On the occasion of the preparations for one Sayyid's wedding party, which I attended, all the names of the guests were written on the side of the letters of invitation. The names of individuals of all social ranks in the Sayyid social hierarchy were clearly and fully written out. When I first carried out my census of the Sayyid population in Jakarta, all names of the Sayyid given to me similarly indicated their social rank. This gave me valuable information on the Sayyid social hierarchy, confirmed by Achmad in Table 4 (1995).[6]

Table 4: Sayyid population by class and *lingkungan* in Cikoang

Lingkungan (Hamlet)	Sayyid Karaeng	Sayyid Tuan	Sayyid Daeng	Number
1. Cikoang	473	851	976	2,300
2. Pattopakkang	327	382	571	1,280
3. Bonto Parang	251	320	358	929
4. Panjangkalang	276	291	326	893
Total	1,327	1,844	2,231	5,402[a]

[a] The total 5,402 is an estimate of the number of all Sayyid in Cikoang.
Source: As compiled from *Catatan Administrasi Imam Kampong Cikoang* (Adapted from Achmad 1995).
NB: Kampong Cikoang has a total population of 8,300 (see Table 1). The figures above indicate that approximately 5,402 or 64.3 per cent of the Cikoangese population are Sayyid. This means that the Jawi comprise only about 2,898 or 35.7 per cent of the total population of Kampong Cikoang. One per cent of 35.7 per cent are Jawi Karaeng, the rest are commoners.

---

5   In reality many young Makassarese, including myself, are reluctant to be called by their Daeng title. They use their *areng paddaengang* (second name) and omit the 'Daeng'; for example, my full name is Muhammad Adlin Daeng Sila (the title was given to me as an infant) but I prefer to answer to Muhammad Adlin Sila.
6   It should be kept in mind that Cikoang is not the only place where the Sayyid of the al-'Aidid clan reside. Jakarta, specifically in Kelurahan Penjaringan in North Jakarta, is another site where I spent two uninterrupted months of my fieldwork (see Chapter Four for the figures of the Sayyid population there).

There is another important indication on which we can rely in order to identify the social order of the Makassarese, including the Sayyid. This is a most visible one, the so-called *sambulayang*, or *timpalaja* in Bugis, of house construction, meaning literally the number of layers in the roof gable; see the illustrations on the following pages.

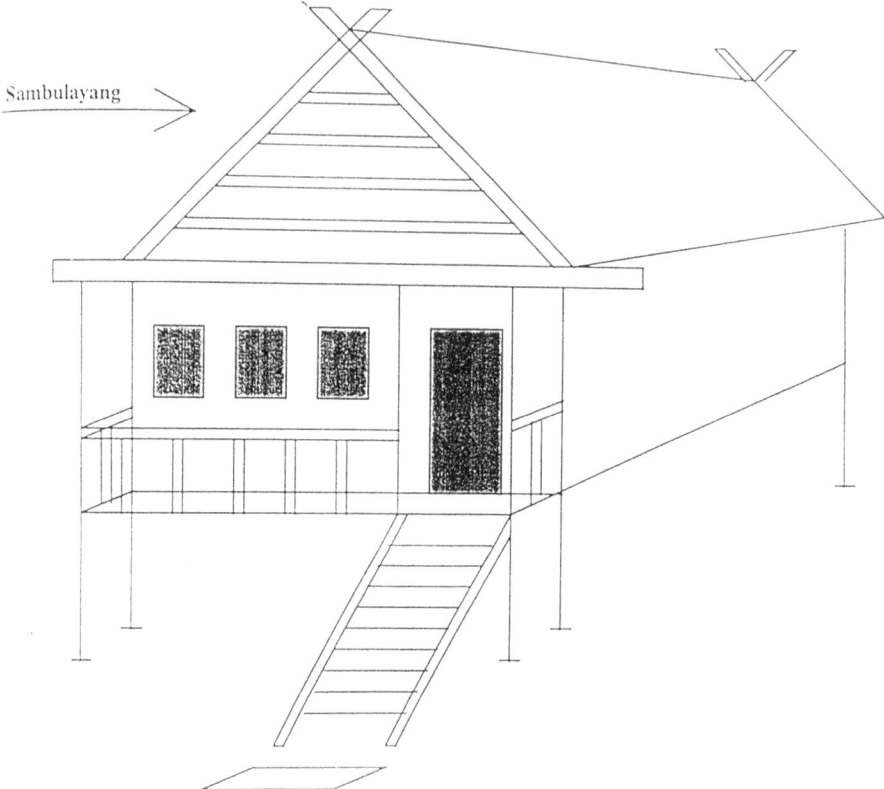

Figure 2: The *sambulayang* indicates the social status of the house owner. The number of layers in the roof gable of this house indicates it belongs to a former Gowa ruler

Figure 3: Balla Lompoa, the house of a former Gowa ruler (Karaeng)

Figure 4: The house of the children of Karaeng (Anakkaraeng)

Figure 5: The house of distinguished people (Tubajik)

Figure 6: The house of commoners (Tusamarak)

3. Origin, Class Status and Socio-cultural Integration in Cikoang

Figure 7: The house of former slaves (Ata)

Figure 8: The playing of drums (*gandrang*)

Normally, the numbers of *sambulayang* are based on the social rank of the householders.⁷ According to Robinson (1996: 1) the basic form of the Makassar house is a 'wooden frame in which a post supports both floor and the roof, which is then finished in a variety of materials.' In modern Makassar, however, as Robinson also found, the construction of houses tends to indicate the degree of prosperity of the householders. The construction is finished as budget permits. Nevertheless, it is the number of *sambulayang* that remains the notable reflection of the social rank of the householders.

The houses of the highest social rank of Makassar's social hierarchy, former Karaeng, the rulers of the kingdom of Gowa, possess the largest number of *sambulayang*: five. The houses of the Anakkaraeng (the nobles) normally have four *sambulayang*, the Tubajik possess three *sambulayang* and the Tusamarak two *sambulayang*, while the houses of the Ata do not have any. This indication, to a certain extent, is not a core distinction of class but it is apparent in terms of the social ranks of Makassar.

As for the Sayyid community, the houses of the Sayyid Karaeng possess the largest number of *sambulayang*; that is, three, similar to those of the Tubajik, and three perhaps because their aristocracy is of lesser rank than the Anakkaraeng (see Bulbeck 1992). The Sayyid Tuan, the Sayyid Daeng and the Jawi Tumaradeka use the same number of *sambulayang*, whereas the house of the Ata in Cikoang are exactly as in other Makassar regions, using no *sambulayang*.

Violations of this architectural hierarchy can cause offence to other social ranks – usually to a higher stratum. If a house of the Jawi Tumaradeka or the Sayyid Daeng, for example, should boast three *sambulayang* (a prerogative of the Sayyid Karaeng and Jawi Karaeng), the head of the *adat* community (e.g. a Sayyid Karaeng) will be the person in charge of settling a possible feud by asking the violator to show proof of his or her Karaeng origin. As I experienced, the violator is not free from punishment, at least the taunts from others, unless he or she can demonstrate genealogical evidence establishing his or her links

---

7   Other indicators are: 1) the playing of the *gandrang* drum at wedding feasts, said to be 'the prerogative of the Makassarese nobility' (Chabot 1996: 112) up to the present time (see Figure 8). All classes within the Sayyid community, as I noted, also play this instrument in wedding celebrations; 2) payment of the *sunrang*, or bride-price, the amount of this given depending on the social stratum of the woman's kin group (Röttger-Rössler 1996: 38).

In principle, the *sunrang* for the women of the Anakkareng is the highest and that of the Ata women the lowest. The Ata women working on the land bring a lower payment than those working inside their Karaeng's house as domestic servants (Sila 1994). Thus the amount of the *sunrang* is established according to rank and status. The figure is always an even number (Chabot 1996: 138). However, a full discussion of the arrangements of the *sunrang* lies beyond the scope of this study.

with the Karaeng. However, such traditional regulations are at present only commonplace in rural areas like Cikoang and are rarely found in the big cities such as Ujung Pandang and Jakarta.[8]

Within the sphere of social interaction, their roles and attributes distinguish the division of the Sayyid from the Jawi, particularly in customary and religious terms. The Sayyid Karaeng are those in charge of maintaining customary law, or *adat*, and often hold the position of *adat* community head. They are also eligible to handle religious practices, such as in the case of H. Maluddin Daeng Sikki al-'Aidid, a Sayyid Karaeng,[9] who usually gives the opening speech and prayer in the Maudu' ceremony which is conducted annually. The Sayyid Tuan and Sayyid Daeng, usually responsible for religious matters, are *anrongguru* or religious teachers. They are normally prepared to be the heads of practices such as the celebration of the Maudu' and the Pattumateang, the ritual purification of the dead, both of which will be further discussed in Chapters Four and Five.

However, it may also happen that the Jawi (particularly the Jawi Karaeng) are also eligible to occupy traditional and religious positions, so long as they obtain an authorisation delegated by a Sayyid as the primary source of authority to become his successors. We see this particularly in religious terms when an *anrongguru* delegates his authority to a Jawi *ana'guru*, his student, whom he intends to become his successor (see Chapter Four).[10]

In summary, the social structure of the Sayyid families in Cikoang is comprised of agnatic lineages because the children inherently take the descent status of their father and not of their mother. This typical tradition has resulted in an exclusive community based on patrilineage (Hisyam 1985). Each patrilineal community is headed by an *opua*, a Sayyid Karaeng, the person in charge of maintaining harmony among the families of the Sayyid.

---

8   In the titular system, the title Sayyid merely indicates descent from the Prophet Muhammad, while al-'Aidid is a family name. As is seen in Table 2, several Sayyid clans are identified by the place they came from. The al-'Aidids originally derived from 'Aidid, a valley situated in the Hadhramaut.

The complicated naming system used by the Sayyid is not uncommon in Cikoang. To give one example: I could call the chairperson of the al-'Aidid Organisation of Makassar and my key informant, Sayyid H. Maluddin al-'Aidid Daeng Sikki, either Karaeng Sikki or simply Daeng Sikki. Sayyid is the marker of his status, H. Maluddin is his given name, al-'Aidid is his lineage name, Sikki is his *areng paddaengang*, Karaeng and Daeng are his Makassarese aristocratic titles.

9   H. Maluddin Daeng Sikki is one of my key informants, whom I regard as my *anrongguru*. Because of his position in the al-'Aidid Organisation, it was from him that I obtained most of my data on the teachings of Sayyid Jalaluddin.

10   This idea of delegation of authority is equally found in Lewis' (1996: 161) ethnography of the Regency of Sikka in East Central Flores.

In 1979, according to a Cikoang source, a more sophisticated association was founded with the title of Kerukunan Keluarga Al-'Aidid (Al-'Aidid Family Harmony). In the next several years, another association was also founded, called IPKA (Ikatan Pemuda Keluarga Al-'Aidid; Al-'Aidid Family Youth Association) which had previously been called IPPA (Ikatan Pemuda Pemudi Al-'Aidid; the Al-'Aidid Youth Association). One of the reasons for the foundation of these associations was, according to my Sayyid informant, to encourage members of families to know each other more closely so that the endogamous marriage system could be properly maintained. Under this system, the number of the Syarifah, regrettably remaining unmarried, will continue to increase unless the Sayyid community provides the means to reduce the number of marriages occurring between Sayyid and non-Syarifah.

The IPKA also sponsors the education of the younger generation of the families in the principles of Sayyid teachings, so that they can maintain their genuineness and be prepared to encounter criticism, especially coming from outsiders, notably the Islamic organisation Muhammadiyah (see Chapter Four). In reality, having more freedom in choosing their partners, the Sayyid men regularly marry non-Syarifah women. This is obvious if we look again at Table 5, where Sayyid Daeng comprise the largest proportion of the population. Far more Sayyid are marrying non-Syarifah than those marrying Syarifah, with the consequence that descendants of the Sayyid and Jawi are now believed to share a mutual culture (Nurdin et al. 1977/1978).

The traces of this process are obvious in modern Cikoang. The Sayyid have adopted many of the Jawi-Makassar social institutions in such matters as notions of social stratification and naming systems, as discussed earlier. In return, the Sayyid traditions of Maudu' and Pattumateang have become the prime religious activities of the Cikoangese as a whole (see Part Two of this study). The Sayyid, with their ascribed status and religious legitimacy, have historically held authority over the Jawi, so that in practice, they participate in a patron–client relationship (Hisyam 1983) (see Chapter Five).

Siri' and *kafa'ah*: Notions of superimposition

According to Makassar-Bugis traditions, apart from the ascription of descent status, the position of people in any social hierarchy is also dependent upon a state called *siri'*. For example, individuals of the Karaeng could fall into slavery if they failed to restore a violated *siri'*, and conversely, individuals of the Tumaradeka could rise to a higher rank if they managed to enhance their *siri'*, or at least maintain their *siri'* stably. *Siri'* is also an inner state with two etymological meanings: the first is shame (In. *malu*) and the second is self-respect, self-worth or self-esteem (In. *martabat* or *harga diri*). Leonard Andaya wrote (1979: 366–367; cf. Marzuki 1995: 115–116):

> The two contradictory meanings of *siri'* must always be kept in balance one with another. By maintaining this equilibrium, a person remains whole, a full individual. If shame should dominate and overwhelm the whole person, then self-respect must bring back into equilibrium. If self-respect should turn to arrogance, then shame or humility should be reasserted to restore the balance. Without the balance of these two aspects of *siri'*, one is considered to be lacking or unwhole.

This inner state is a standard measure for crediting the value of a person within the Makassar notion of personhood. Once one's *siri'* is offended the person will feel embarrassed (Mak. *ripakasiri'*) until he can restore it. Otherwise, he might be considered as a lesser person (Mak. *tenasiri'na*). To be a whole person (Mak. *tautojeng*) means to keep the *siri'* in stability (Mak. *paentengi siri'nu*).

External causes of embarrassment vary in the present day, but previously they referred only to women's misbehaviour. In older times, but still commonplace now mainly in rural areas, it was taboo for a woman, particularly if she was officially engaged, to be seen sitting or walking with another man (intentionally or unintentionally) without the full knowledge of her family. Chabot (1996: 182) best illustrates this phenomenon:

> A young girl only leaves the house in the company of older women. Little excursions are holidays for her. She dresses carefully for these occasions, she makes herself up, blackens her eyebrows and the hairline on her forehead, and powders her face. The older women guard and protect her. In their presence, a young girl is safe. If she is alone at home or in the yard and a man enters the yard accidentally, a dangerous situation is created because this encounter, regardless of the intention of both parties, is considered a breach of the established forms of social intercourse. If a neighbour woman were to see and talk about it, so that the girl's brother hears of it, the latter would feel *siri'* and act accordingly.

The family of the girl, especially her kinsmen, would feel shamed by such a deed. In such a situation, they are called *tumassiri'*, literally the 'offended' party. In another case, if a girl were to decide to marry a man without the permission of her family, her *annyala* (In. *kawin lari*) or elopement dissolves any engagement already arranged by her family. The girl then brings dishonour upon the family, causes their humiliation and undermines the *siri'* of the family as a whole (Marzuki 1995: 35; Chabot 1996: 236–255).

There are three kinds of *annyala*: *silariang*, where both the girl and the man agree to elope; *nilariang*, where the girl is abducted by the man and finds an *imam* in charge of Islamic marriages to marry them (usually due to the refusal of the girl's family to the man's prior marriage proposal); and *erangkale*, where the girl forces the man to marry, partly due to sexual advances which sometimes lead to pregnancy, by reporting the man's deed to the *imam* so that he is obliged to marry her. *Annyala*, in any of its three types, does not seek the approval of the families involved. It is considered to be the last resort after other normal processes have proved unsuccessful. Similarly, it is used when both parties already understand that approval of their marriage is impossible, most often due to differences in the social rank. I met one Syarifah who decided to choose *annyala*, because her chosen fiancé was a non-Sayyid.

On the other hand, in the past the consequences of breaking an agreed betrothal to take on another partner was traditionally death for both the girl and the young man because such was considered to be the remedy to cure offended *siri'*. One of the methods of alternative reconciliation is called *abbajik* (Mak; Ind. *perdamaian*) or 'making peace'. If the young man's parents asked for *abbajik* from the girl's family and their apology was accepted, with the payment of compensation by the man or his family, then *appasala*, or the death penalty would not come into effect.

The *abbajik* involves a representative of both the girl and man being sent to the family of the girl to offer the peace proposal. The process may continue through a number of further meetings, and successful negotiation depends partly on the credibility and integrity of the representatives. Such categories as the descent, wealth and social rank of the representatives can guarantee that resolution is achieved. Once peace is restored, an official approval of the forthcoming marriage is then made known openly to all the girl's relatives, including the family of her former fiancé, in the hope that it can restore the violated *siri'* of her family. On the other hand, if the proposal fails the young man and the girl must go into exile until their proposal can be accepted over time.

For the Sayyid, however, there is no such word as forgiveness in their dictionary. Once a woman of the Sayyid house behaves in such a way she will be isolated from her kin group. Yet, unlike the ordinary Makassarese, the Sayyid do not show their anger by exercising the death penalty upon the transgressors of their *siri'* since, according to one Sayyid, there is no cure for that kind of violation. The most the woman will receive is the loss of familial ties with her relatives for an unspecified period of time.

In the eyes of the Makassarese, the Bugis and the Sayyid, the position of women is the predominant factor that influences the *siri'* of the family. Chabot's analysis (1996) is that men are the defender of *siri'* while women are the 'vessels' or 'bearers' of *siri'*. According to Makassar and Bugis traditions (especially among the Karaeng) it is preferred for women to marry men according to their family's arrangements, when they will be selected from the same stratum or a higher stratum, or those who are distinguished by their wealth (Mak. *tukalumannyang*), intelligence (Mak. *tucara'de*), bravery in war (Mak. *tubarani*) or trustworthiness (Mak. *tubajik*). Thus the preferred tendency of the Makassar women to marry 'up' is the typical pattern of marriage in the region.

In normal situations for the Sayyid, however, the Syarifah must marry a man of equal descent to themselves. The Syarifah must marry a man of Sayyid origin, regardless of his social capacity such as wealth, intelligence, moral qualities and so forth. For example, the Syarifah Karaeng are allowed to marry Sayyid Daeng, or beneath themselves, so long as the man is a Sayyid.

Among the Makassarese, a bride-price, locally called *sunrang*, a gift of the groom to the bride (usually a specified amount of money), is one of the most meaningful elements of marriage tradition, because the amount of the *sunrang* signifies dignity of social rank. A different perspective is to be found in the Sayyid community, where the *sunrang* is not so important, indeed not necessary so long as there is a Sayyid man available to marry their Syarifah. One Sayyid Karaeng told me:

> Usually, a man cannot afford to meet the amount of *sunrang* required by the Makassarese girl's family. This sometimes leads to the failure of a marriage proposal. We the Sayyid are not like that, because marriage between our children is more important. We even assist a man of Sayyid descent financially if he is poor, to enable him to proceed with the desired marriage.

Among the Buginese and Makassarese the *siri'* of the young women and their family will be enhanced by marriage to a distinguished man, because such a union will put their offspring in a higher place in the social hierarchy than ever before. If the reverse is the case, the women will decrease their family's *siri'* and cause offence. The most common way for families to preserve the stability of *siri'* is by exercising endogamous marriage. This is done through bilateral lines, where the prospective husband and wife are derived from bilineal descent on both the father's and mother's sides, commonly known as cross-cousin marriage. Thus the *siri'* of the Makassarese and Bugis family is significantly dependent upon the standing of the daughter's future partner.[11]

In modern times, the question of *siri'* involves more varied situations; for instance, I found cases in other parts of Makassar where a village head would feel humiliated if asked to step down from office. 'It is a matter of *siri''* said one, 'therefore I insist on maintaining this office.' Another example is that a father will feel humiliated or embarrassed if his children fail to perform well in school. Thus, *siri'* is to some extent currently to do with the social status of a person or a family in society. The better the material living standards, the higher the *siri'*

---

11   This information was given in an interview with Bapak Abu Hamid in Ujung Pandang.

of a family will also be, and vice versa. The death penalty imposed on errant young people in their choice of marriage partner, previously considered to be a remedy for *siri'* violation, is no longer generally apparent among the Bugis and Makassarese.

As for the Sayyid, they will feel humiliated (Mak. *tumassiri'*) or become 'shamed persons' if they cannot afford to celebrate their traditional rites such as the Maudu' festival, while violation against their distinctive marriage tradition of *kafa'ah* is still considered to be the most severe attack on their *siri'*. For the Sayyid there is nothing more worthy of protection in this world than *kafa'ah*.

Bloodline, then, is the chief principle of Sayyid family identity. In order to preserve their pure line with its ties with the Prophet, the Sayyid strive to exercise *kafa'ah* strictly in their policy of marriage. *Kafa'ah* has a root meaning in Arabic of 'equal' or 'proper' (and hence 'equality of marriage partner') and thus refers to marriage between the Sayyid and the Syarifah. Prospective husbands and wives who can both show blood ties with the household of Muhammad are always considered to be the best arranged partners.

Within more general Cikoangese social interaction this kind of marriage points to a distinction held between the Sayyid and the non-Sayyid, the Jawi Makassarese. With the identification of their origins, the Sayyid regard themselves as of superior worth. Bloodline becomes a metaphor for the quality and value of their family. This idea of bloodline is also the primary metaphor for honour. Absence of a genealogical link with the Prophet implies a lower moral worth. These principles, then, define the Sayyids' identity and the quality of their relations with other people (cf. Abu-Lughod 1986).

The identification of nobility of origin reflects the ideological system of the Sayyid. The Sayyid social structure is comprised of agnatic lineage, with descent traced through males. This explains why the preferred type of marriage is patrilateral parallel cousin marriage, 'the combination of husband and wife coming from their father's side', or marriage between two brothers' children. Many acknowledgements of the soundness of this marriage system are reported by my informants, particularly regarding matters of raising the children, taking care of the property of the husband and even more importantly, observing the Sayyid's long standing traditions. About this, my Sayyid informant told me.

> A Syarifah wife is better, because there is no need to teach her the significance of Maudu' and how to perform it, because she already knows. There is no complaint anymore when the money is running out because of financing the Maudu'. Nevertheless, if the wife is not a Syarifah, it is very difficult to make her understand the significance of Maudu'; she even can drive us mad.

According to Sayyid Maluddin, in principle, a Sayyid is only permitted to marry a woman of another (i.e. lower) stratum if he has first married a Syarifah. After this, a Sayyid can marry others; yet in the field I found hardly any statistics or percentages of the first marriage in cases of polygyny. Such marriages are allowed because the capacity of the Sayyid as *pannongkoki*, literally, 'patron and carrier' of the Sayyid blood. When the Sayyid marry women from other strata the children of this union will be honoured equally as Sayyid, the children taking the descent status of their father. This tradition is quite similar to what Bujra observes in the Hadhramaut (1971: 93):

> As interpreted by the Sadah (plural of Sayyid) in Hadhramaut, *kafa'ah* is held to refer to equality of descent only, and they have supported this interpretation with religious arguments and their power in society. Thus, they argue that a man ought to marry one of equal descent status to himself, but that if no such suitable spouse exists he may marry a woman of lower descent. Such a marriage is allowed because the children will take the descent status of their father and not their mother.

Within their social interaction, women of the Anakkaraeng or lower stratum, having been married by the Sayyid, can be fully accepted as part of his kin group, so long as they live together with the kin for a lengthy period. The female outsiders, with their children, can be part of the Sayyid family through marriage if they can fully familiarise and adjust themselves as members of the kin in all aspects of life.

The term 'familiarisation' is also significant in the kinship system of the Sayyid. Particularly for the non-Syarifah women married to Sayyid, living in the surrounds of the Sayyid community after marriage is most preferred, so that they can fully participate in the Sayyid traditional practices, which in turn can strengthen their relationship to one another. To quote a phrase taken from one of my informants: *'Manna bija punna bellai pammantanganna, taumaraenji antu rikatte'* ('Even if they are members of our relatives but live far away from us, they can be regarded as foreigners') (see Hisyam 1985). So we see that the Sayyid kinship system is not only patrilineal but also patrilocal.

In terms of marriage, affinal kin are also important to the Sayyid community. Intermarriage between the Sayyid and the non-Syarifah associates agnatic and affinal ties (the descendants of the union being categorised as either Sayyid Karaeng or Sayyid Daeng). This is also what Radcliffe-Brown (1971: 129) found in Africa, that a marriage is not just a 'union of a man and a woman; it is an alliance between two families or bodies of kin'.

The agnatic tie is called *bija pammanakang*, or 'all male relatives' – defined as kindred in anthropological terminology as an ego-centred network of bilateral ties. That is to say, it is a culturally recognised category of bilateral relatives, which may extend only to a certain degree of relationship from ego (e.g. until third cousins). The affinal tie is termed *bija panrenrengang*, which covers all relatives who enter the kin group through marriage. Both these categories, *bija pammanakang* and *bija panrenrengang* play an important role in the realm of the policy of marital unions, because whom one is allowed to marry is assessed in terms of *bija pammanakang*. From the viewpoint of the Sayyid traditions, all relatives inheriting Sayyid blood (by kindred or lineage) are categorised as *bija pammanakang*.

For the non-Sayyid societies of Makassar, the term *bija pammanakang* refers to those who can trace descent through both male and female, or bilineal/ambilineal links (see Chabot 1996). Keesing (1975) has proposed the term 'cognatic descent' to refer to those systems which trace descent through male and female links indiscriminately. For the nobles, who do focus on their ancestors, one can speak of cognatic descent, whereas commoners tend to be organised merely in networks based on kindred. However, current patron–client relations tend to shade these distinctions, as commoners also tend to claim a relationship of descent with nobles of previous generations, i.e. Karaeng.

On the other hand, the right of an individual to obtain a Sayyid title is allocated through his or her father's side, a principle that allows us to speak of patrilineal descent. Unlike the boys, once girls are born within a *bija pammanakang* group, they are directed to choose their partner from *bija pammanakang* only. This idea of *bija pammanakang*, I think, is the real framework of the *kafa'ah* system (see Appendix III).

Diagram 3: Patrilineal descent

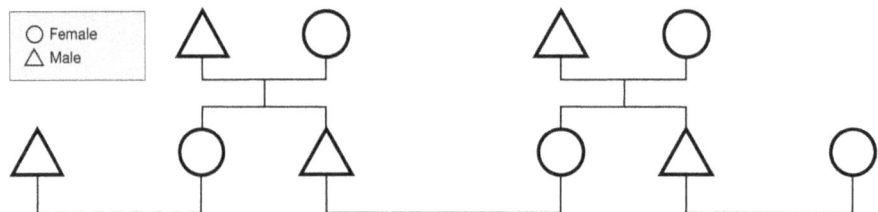

NB: The dotted lines indicate that the marriage is not allowed (Syarifah with non-Sayyid).

As a corollary, it is due to the greater freedom given to the Sayyid men that many complaints have come from the Syarifah who have no possibility of choosing their own partners from another social stratum. Many Syarifah told me that they have to choose either to become a *tulolo bangko*, an old maid, when few

Sayyid are available to marry them,[12] or to ignore the long-standing tradition of *kafa'ah* system by eloping with non-Sayyid men by *annyala*. If they choose the latter, the consequences will be severe; they still remember that it was once punishable by death.

This situation relates to the idea of modesty. According to my Sayyid informants, modesty is attributed to femininity while *siri'*, as self-respect, self-worth and self-esteem, is associated with masculinity. Yet through the path of modesty, a Syarifah can obtain or even enhance her *siri'* and that of her family by strictly following the rules of the *kafa'ah* system. She can maintain her status, the blood link with the household of the Prophet Muhammad and at the same time enhance her own personal worth. The reverse choice will raise a so-called *ammere'*, a 'violation' against *kafa'ah* (see Hisyam 1985), which in turn undermines the *siri'* of her family. In a taped interview with a Syarifah maiden I was told that if a Syarifah tries to manipulate the law, she will put herself at a terrible risk. Her family will be marked with the shame of *tumassiri'* and become 'offended' people. Her family would no longer want to recognise her as its daughter and upon her death would not even pray for her.

My informants further told me that normally the Sayyid never asked to be honoured but that local people always pay conspicuous respect to them by, for example, bowing before the Sayyid or kissing the Sayyid's right hand whenever and wherever they meet him. If, however, people do not behave in this way, it will not offend the Sayyid. In the first several weeks of my contact with the Cikoangese, I could not distinguish the Sayyid and Jawi from one another. Yet the Sayyid never asked me to change my attitude to them – until I found out for myself what were the prevailing protocols of etiquette.

---

12   The idea of the *tulolo bangko* is also widespread among the women of the Anakkaraeng and Tubajik in the non-Sayyid Makassarese societies who prefer to marry distinguished men. They, like the unmarried Syarifah, usually live in the house of their married brothers and sisters to become caretakers of the house and the children.

PART TWO

CHAPTER FOUR

The Ideological Dimensions of Disputes over Religious Practices in Cikoang

In this chapter I will examine certain current religious arguments over popular beliefs and practices of the Muslims of Cikoang. In Cikoang there are many scholars and teachers constituting religion as a definable sphere of knowledge and practice, with the people identifying themselves with one of two chief religious orientations. The first is that of the so-called 'Cikoangese' (Mak. *tu Cikoang*; In. *orang Cikoang*) consisting of the Sayyid and Jawi people, but practically grouped as one social unit through the relationships of Sayyid patrons and Jawi clients, with their similar long-standing socio-religious practices discussed in the previous chapter. They identify themselves as those who affirm long-standing religious practices inherited from Sayyid Jalaluddin and his successors while associating themselves with a specific school of Islamic institutions.

Those of the second orientation have come to be known as 'outsiders' (Mak. *tu pantara*; Ind. *orang luar*). As mentioned earlier, this category may also include some Cikoangese themselves, both Sayyid and Jawi. I use the term 'outsiders' to refer to those who argue against the distinctive Cikoangese festivities of Maudu' and Pattumateang. For the main, they have obtained their religious knowledge through modern educational institutions such as those owned by the organisation Muhammadiyah[1] and they include those who have graduated from other networks of schools and associations supported by the Islamic modernist movement.

Here in this second part of the study I group the two clusters of Muslims into the categories of 'traditionalists' and 'modernists'.[2] The Cikoangese tend to regard themselves in most respects as traditionalists, to the extent that their religious specialists (the Sayyid, along with a small number of Jawi) perpetuate their traditional knowledge of beliefs and practices and counter any kind of criticism from outsiders. On the other hand, the adherents of the modernist movement may reside both in or beyond the village of Cikoang. These are mostly said to be non-Sayyid, with a small number of Jawi and Sayyid who have graduated from educational institutions outside Sayyid control.

In terms of the present analysis, I propose a way of viewing the typical roles of the two groups as they have been identified and expounded upon by Makassar scholars in particular and by Indonesian scholars in general. The two categories have also frequently attracted internal discussion, not only in Cikoang but also in Ujung Pandang and Jakarta, which constitute the three regions of Cikoangese residence.

My fieldwork was longer in Jakarta than in Cikoang and Ujung Pandang. I stayed in Jakarta for more than two months out of the four months of my gathering of data because it was there that I had more access to a number of Sayyid who were facing religious criticism from non-Sayyid people: not only from non-Sayyid Makassarese but also from other Indonesians – Javanese, Betawi, Sundanese and Minangkabau – who personally supported the modernist movement. Some Sayyid experienced opposition directly, while others heard it reported by their elders. Some had had personal experience of the religious debate with the Muhammadiyah in Cikoang and Ujung Pandang regions as well.

In the following discussion we shall see how these Cikoangese protect their identity, even as it changes within the context of their social relations with other Muslims in Jakarta. The basic aim is to explore the extent to which the Cikoangese in Jakarta maintain adherence to their religious practices in the face of the challenges of the modernists.

---

1 'One of the most important Muslim social organisations in Indonesia in the prewar period, perhaps until the modern time. It was founded in Yogyakarta on 18 November 1912 by Kyahi Haji Ahmad Dahlan in response to suggestions made by his pupils. Its aim was the spreading of Islam among the population and the promotion of religious life among its members. For this purpose it was to establish educational institutions, *waqf* (charities), mosques and published books, brochures, newspapers and periodicals.' Noer 1973: 75.

2 I have adopted these useful terms from the perspective of John R. Bowen's study in the Gayo highlands; they may have different manifestations in the context of Cikoang and other communities, as Bowen has acknowledged (Bowen 1993).

And changes have taken place, in part due to the small numbers of the Sayyid population in the region, which is the reverse of the situation in Cikoang. At present many young Cikoangese receive their devotional learning from other domains, which has broadened their religious horizons (see Table 5 below). Consequently, there is both space for religious reform and a new appreciation of their traditions by young Cikoangese which is flexible and tolerant. Even so, these changes may bring only variations – without radical implications – for the authenticity of their traditions. In Jakarta, specifically in Kelurahan Penjaringan situated in North Jakarta, I chose as my population sample Luar Batang, one of Kelurahan Penjaringan's two hamlets, the other being Muara Baru.

Table 5: Sayyid population by class in Luar Batang hamlet, Kelurahan Penjaringan, North Jakarta, 1996

Variable	Number	Per cent
Sayyid Karaeng	2	0.4
Sayyid Tuan	31	6.4
Sayyid Daeng	14	2.9
Non-Sayyid peoples (the Jawi and other Makassar from Turratea regions, Takalar and Jeneponto).	438	90.3
Total	485[a]	100

[a] The total 485 is taken from Kantor Kelurahan Penjaringan Jakarta Utara (1996).

I was able to explore the extent to which one of the largest modernist organisations, Muhammadiyah, managed to interact socially with the Cikoangese in this area. It is my purpose here to reach a general understanding of religious beliefs and proper practices constructed and debated by these two categories of Muslims.[3]

Traditionalists versus modernists

When I first arrived in the Makassar settlement in the Kelurahan, or sub-district, of Penjaringan, North Jakarta, I had not intended to explore religious arguments between traditionalists and modernists. Instead, I had planned to observe how the Makassarese there maintained their kinship system after a long

---

3   I prefer to use the terms 'beliefs' and 'practices' rather than adopting Kluckhon's (1965: 45–79) 'myth' and 'ritual' because, according to the two groups of Muslims, there is no valid separation between the Islamic doctrines they embrace and the practices they perform. For them, there is unity in faith and action: their practices are an expression of their faith, or what Graham (1983: 59) viewed as 'a symbolic articulation of Muslim ideals and values'. Rippin (1990: 99) also observed a lack of mythological sense in any of the Muslim rituals; they are 'an expression of an individual's piety and obedience to God's command and an indication of the person's membership within the Islamic community'.

period of emigration from home. Yet the ongoing debate between these two groups of Muslims soon drew me to discover the substance of the two camps' opposing religious orientations.

On a November day in 1996, when beginning to collect my census, I dropped by a branch office of Muhammadiyah located in the centre of the hamlet of Luar Batang. I was curious about the extent to which Muhammadiyah had managed to survive in the very typical Cikoangese area, whereas in Cikoang itself Muhammadiyah had never been able to put down roots, because of a strong resistance by the local people (see below). Pak Darul, who is the Deputy Chairman of the Muhammadiyah sub-branch founded in 1979, admitted to me:

> Here (in Luar Batang) in order not to be rejected, we never present any of the Muhammadiyah attributes in approaching the Cikoangese. We facilitate classes open to children only (mostly the children of the Cikoangese) for practice in reciting the Qur'an and the teaching of religious studies. Children are easier to teach than their parents, who are already too fanatical about their traditions. We hope that these children will have a better knowledge of their religion in the future.

Pak Darul then introduced me to one of his former students who is now very keen to support the modernist movement of Muhammadiyah. Pak Darul's acknowledgement above, and several interviews conducted with him after that, brought me to two conclusions: first, that the Muhammadiyah never put their views into public contest with the Cikoangese; second, because neither of the two parties is brave enough to criticise the other openly, it being a very sensitive matter, they seem to live in harmony. However, the two camps' opposing ideas over what constitutes Islamic belief and how religious practices should be carried out became apparent when I conducted a series of confidential interviews, projective tests and other psychological testing methods on a number of members of the two groups (see Keesing 1982: 31). The ethnographic data presented here are a result of that research.

Before I explore the views of the modernists, it needs to be pointed out that within the traditionalist group itself there also exists an argument between the Sayyid, who hold religious authority, and the Jawi people. Early research (see Hisyam 1985) showed that this debate is a result of the patron–client relationship between them. This long-standing relationship has practically always benefited the Sayyid. With their economic, traditional and religious authority, the Sayyid present themselves as being more honourable and as having higher moral worth than the Jawi. In return, according to the Jawi people I spoke with, the daily actions of the Sayyid are expected to be exemplary. As descendants of the Prophet, the Sayyid should behave in a manner similar to his life. Yet in reality, say the Jawi people, many Sayyid are habitually the same as themselves – less pious Muslims. It was not uncommon for the Jawi and the outsiders to mention this matter to me – but they did so in private.

The Sayyid principally base their view of proper conduct on the scriptures of the Qur'an and Hadith or accounts of the Prophet's behaviour. However, according to the Jawi, there are Sayyid who also transgress certain prohibitions, while always, the Jawi argue, excusing their conduct in ways in which fundamentally run counter to the teachings of Islam and to common sense. One Jawi told me:

> I found one Sayyid who was drunk on alcohol, and when I asked him why he drank (because Islam forbids alcoholic beverages) he replied, 'I am a Sayyid and a descendant of the Prophet, my blood is pure. Whether I am drunk or not, it does not matter, I will stay clean from sin.'

This is one among numerous other examples which lead the Jawi to question the origins of the Sayyid as true descendants of the Prophet. Such doubt, and many other criticisms which I heard voiced, indicate that some Jawi have been moved either intentionally or unintentionally to support the modernist movement.

And yet it is a fact that the Sayyid rely on the Jawi in a different form of dependency, that is, for their religious domination. Without the Jawi in subjection to them the religious legitimacy of the Sayyid becomes less powerful. The Sayyid need the support of the Jawi for the maintenance of their integrity. The relative numbers of the Sayyid population can also be another parameter of the lessening of Jawi subjection to the Sayyid. Since the proportion of their population is much smaller in Jakarta than in Cikoang, the Jawi in Jakarta have had far greater freedom in their religious activities, so that the Sayyid are no longer the only religious specialists accessible to the Jawi.

Nevertheless, as Hisyam (1985) observed, this doubt about Sayyid origins and their religious licence has not affected the belief of the Jawi in the teachings of the Sufi Tarekat Bahr ul-Nur and in their honouring of the Prophet. Enthusiasm for celebrating the Maudu' festival is still very much alive among them. The Jawi only expect consistency in the everyday speech and actions of the Sayyid as their religious specialists.[4]

Another factor giving rise to religious argument is the fact that among the Jawi there are a number who have experienced wider horizons. This group of educated Jawi, along with Muhammadiyah in general, challenge the provenance of the Sayyids' Islamic beliefs and practices. Yet official or institutional attempts to criticise openly the teachings of traditionalists are rare. Rather, debates arise in private contexts. This is so because critics are in fear of violating the well-

---

4 See Hisyam (1985: 28–30) for a discussion of other reasons for the conflict.

being of the social body as a whole. Meanwhile, it is the teachers, scholars and students of educational institutions who are mostly *tu pantara*, or outsiders, who have produced scholarly written criticisms.[5]

The main principle of the modernist position is the belief that each individual Muslim should take responsibility for understanding the scriptures, the Qur'an and Hadith. In their religious practices, all Muslims, traditionalists and modernists alike, always recognise that the Syari'at and the scriptures are the God-prescribed 'path' for humans to follow. These are the centre of their faith and the source of the doctrines and duties that all good Muslims must try to observe and apply in their daily conduct. In relation to the mystical beliefs of *tasawuf* and the Tarekat Bahr ul-Nur, modernists do not agree with such practices, which focus unduly on the Prophet Muhammad (cf. Schimmel 1985). They see most Sufi teachers as giving an exaggerated image of his character. Modernists make clear that the axis of Islam is not the figure of Muhammad; rather, it is the message that God sent to humankind through him, whether collected as the Qur'an or embodied in his 'statements' and 'actions' recorded in the Hadith.[6] In other words, modernists agree that it is understandable if Muslims are fond of praising the Prophet because he is the father of the *ummah*, the Muslim community, but what is most important is to what extent Muslims appreciate and put into practice in their daily lives the messages revealed by God.

In addition, say the modernists, despite every religious matter having its own justification in scripture, we should use our power of reason. We should critically observe every religious practice. We can use other written religious texts for reference, but they are applicable only to the extent that they clarify what already appears in scripture. Changing what scripture reveals or practising what scripture has never ordered is perceived as heretical innovation, called in Arabic, *bid'ah*. For this reason, the modernists stress the importance of correctly interpreting scripture.

In so doing, continue the modernists, should there be those in doubt about one single statement of scripture, we need reliable scholars to prevent them from interpreting freely on their own (see Bowen 1993). Modernists often quote the Prophet Muhammad to the effect that 'anyone who performs what I never give

---

5   On the celebration of Maulid in Cikoang, see Ahmad 1979/1980; Gassing 1975; Malik 1997. All of the writers are graduates of the State Institute for Islamic Studies (IAIN) of Ujung Pandang.
6   John Bowen (1993: 22) explains: 'the reports (Hadith) were written down only after they had been transmitted orally across several generations, and religious scholars have evaluated them in part by scrutinising the reliability of each link in the chain of transmission. Deciding on the correctness of a particular religious practice often turns on the reliability – itself to be judged from the moral character of each transmitter.' See also Juynboll (1983) and Fischer and Abedi (1990: 95–149).

as an example, the reward of his or her doing is refused'. Thus a person may do everything as he or she wishes, except where it is unlawful in Islam or without prophetic precedent to do so.

The traditionalists also stand for what they feel is right in principle from the scriptural sources. They often justify their customary beliefs and practices by referring to the Hadith traditionally recorded by past scholars. In the series of interviews which I held with Cikoangese traditionalists, I was personally impressed by their ability to justify their practices. They appeared to be well equipped in their knowledge of scripture. Many of them – almost all Sayyid and a small number of Jawi – are familiar with Qur'anic verses and Hadith and know how to recite them, mostly in Indonesian and Makassarese. Yet this knowledge tends to be limited to certain matters, such as the grounds for conducting the Maudu' festival.

Such differences in the interpretation and elucidation of the texts of the Qur'an and Hadith adopted by these two groups of Muslims serve their opposing positions. For the modernists, scripture may have only one set of conventional interpretations. These are the vernacular renderings called *tafsir,* which contain interpretations of and commentaries of scripture pioneered by later scriptural scholars (Ar. *mufassir*). The most popular source used by the majority of today's Muslims, both Sunni and Shi'i, is the highly influential 30-volume *Fi Zilal al-Qur'an* (In the Shadow of the Qur'an) by the Egyptian thinker Sayyid Qutb (d. 1386/1966) of Egypt's Muslim Brotherhood (see Ayoub 1984: 7).

On the other hand, the traditionalists rely on the interpretations of the Qur'an and Hadith inherited from religious specialists of the more distant past, which have been handed down orally from generation to generation. The traditionalists faithfully perpetuate the sayings and actions of the earlier scholars and feel isolated from their comrades when they no longer show appreciation of the precedents of old. The bottom line is that the utilisation of *tafsir* is the concern of the modernists only, so that the traditionalists have come to conceive of *tafsir* as a symbol of the modernist movement.

Many times during my fieldwork I heard the opinion by the modernists that most scriptural references cited by the traditionalists are, in modern scholarly terminology, *da'if,* 'weak', and sometimes even *maudu',* 'false', being based on an unreliable or a non-conventional understanding. For instance, one of the Hadith which I collected from the traditionalists states: 'The Prophet Muhammad said: someone is not yet regarded as among the true believers before he loves me more than he loves himself, his parents, his children and his descendants.' According to the interpretation of the traditionalists, in order to show love and admiration to the Prophet, Muslims are obligated to celebrate the day of his birth. In weddings and the Pattumateang, or ritual purification of dead souls, for example, the traditionalists prefer to perform Barazanji, songs of praise, to the person of the Prophet over recitation of the Qur'an.

In addition, both modernists and traditionalists seem to consider the ongoing debates between them to arise from different Islamic schools of thought (Ar. *madhhab*), which they both legally adopt. We know that the majority of Indonesian Muslims follow the Madhhab Safi'i, a Sunni law school which counsels reliance on the collective practices of Syari'at (the Qur'an and Hadith). The traditionalists of Cikoang adopt the Madhhab Ahl ul-Bait (School of Members of the Prophet's House, i.e. his descendants), which stresses the knowledge of *tasawuf* via the Tarekat Bahr ul-Nur. One Sayyid Daeng explained to me:

> We (the Sayyid) are more interested in studying *tasawuf* (rather than Syari'at) because it is the essence of Islam. *Tasawuf* for us is like the extracted rich milk of the coconut fruit (In. *santan*), while Syari'at is just like its outer husk (In. *sabuk kelapa*). It is the *santan* which is the core of the coconut and not the *sabuk kelapa*.

Traditionally, knowledge of *tasawuf* is transmitted orally by an *anrongguru* to the *ana'guru*. It was only recently, in 1996, that Maluddin Daeng Sikki, head of the al-'Aidid Organisation of Makassar recorded the doctrine in writing.

However, both groups have come to suggest that Muslims should attempt more to rise above conflict. *Khilafiyah*, or different interpretations of scripture over specifically detailed problems, should never be contested, but rather their variety must be understood as *rachmat*, God's mercy. Although this latter statement, pushed harder by the traditionalists, is reluctantly tolerated by the modernists, it has currently become a unifying cry for Muslims in discussions of religious life in Cikoang.

The religious orientations of the traditionalists

As we saw earlier, the teachings of Sayyid Jalaluddin al-'Aidid were continued by his children and a number of his students such as the historical figures Hapeleka, noted for his memorisation of the Qur'an and Sayyid Abdullah As-Saqqaf (or Asseggaf). In particular, Hapeleka recorded the details of Sayyid Jalaluddin's doctrine in specially written prayers called *jikkiri* (Mak.; from Ar. and In. *zikir*, remembrance) covering the celebration of the Maudu' festival and supplying the religious grounds of it. These Jikkiri were collected in a book known as *Bayanul Bayan* and signed by Sayyid Jalaluddin himself in 1032 AH/1632 CE (see Nurdin et al. 1977/1978: 38; Hisyam 1985: 19). The manuscript is still kept in Eastern Cikoang, in Kampong Lakatong (see maps on page 18 of this volume) under the guardianship of the descendants of Hapeleka. It cannot be disclosed to any unknown or unreliable people, because of its sacredness.[7]

Despite the fact that, as Hamonic (1985) has argued, there is a group of people in Cikoang who consciously consider themselves to be Shi'i Muslims, a large part of the religious doctrines circulating in Cikoang are based on the cosmological conception of Nur Muhammad, the Divine Light of Muhammad coeval with creation, which is not a specification of the doctrine of the Shi'ah as such, but of *tasawuf*, both ideologically and terminologically speaking. According to my findings, the Cikoangese also do not traditionally celebrate the martyrdom of Husein on the 10th day of Muharram as do other Shi'i Indonesians, such as takes place in the *tabot* festival held in Bengkulu and certain Minangkabau areas of Sumatra. This is what the traditionalists of Cikoang believe:

> We (the Sayyid) consider ourselves as followers of the Shi'ah in terms of our marriage policy, *kafa'ah*. This system is essentially viewed as Shi'ah, whereas other beliefs and practices are Sunni, while the Maudu' festival alone is the Cikoangese typical ritual. We are not able to reproduce exactly the doctrine practiced in Iran (a Shi'ah state) such as in terms of leadership (i.e. the Imamate or rule by learned clergy) which should be both secular and under ritual chiefs, because we cannot impose our expectations on the society where we reside. We tend to assimilate, that is how we introduce Islam to the local people; we marry the local women, then Islam is introduced to them.

This acknowledgement would seem to be disingenuous, because in fact the Sayyid dominate the current administration of the Cikoang bureaucracy; for example, the head of Mangarabombang district, a higher authority than the Cikoang village head, is genealogically a Sayyid Karaeng (see Diagram 2).

The question of Shi'ism is not the main concern of the modernists; rather it is the method in which the traditionalist ritual practices are conducted which the modernists, for the most part, take issue with. Hence I am more concerned with how the Cikoangese Muslims decide their methods of understanding doctrine in relation to the Maudu' festival, rather than arguing whether or not Shi'ah ideology either underlies or is superimposed upon the religious orientation of the Muslims of Cikoang.[8]

For the Sayyid, Tarekat Bahr ul-Nur is another name for the doctrine of Nur Muhammad that the light of Muhammad's prophecy was coeval with the creation of the Qur'an and with creation itself. Taught by Sayyid Jalaluddin

---

7 Karaeng Sikki informed me that an attempt had been made to photograph this core manuscript of the Tarekat Bahr ul-Nur. When the film was printed it was blank. References which I use here are from derived sources owned by Karaeng Sikki.
8 Compare Hamonic 1985: 180.

and his successors, it serves as the primary ground of the religious orientation of the traditionalists. They maintain that this *tarekat* originates from their Madhhab Ahl ul-Bait, and to counter modernist criticism, they emphasise their religious practices as the valid enactment of the Madhhab Ahl ul-Bait.[9] In terms of the beliefs and practices of Tarekat Bahr ul-Nur, if we enquire as to why a certain teaching is set out in a particular way (especially in relation to the Maudu' festival) the traditionalists say: 'We repeat the old stories in the way they were told to us and with the words we ourselves remember.' Their defence obeys the idea of *taqlid* in Islam. Strictly speaking, *taqlid* refers to the uncritical acceptance of legal and theological decisions of a teacher or teachers, or simply the unquestioning following of tradition. It is anathema to the modernist position. 'To follow *taqlid* is *bid'ah,* it is heretical innovation in religion', say the modernists, since in *taqlid* there is no attempt on the part of the traditionalists to refer to scripture for validation or clarification.

The modernists, in their opposition to *taqlid,* emphasise the exercise of individual reason, called *ijtihad*; that is, the process of checking and rechecking the interpretation of scripture used to justify a particular practice, rather than blindly following earlier sayings and actions of the elders. The modernists maintain that every Muslim should understand and implement Islamic teachings by using *ijtihad* if capable of doing so; if not, a Muslim then exercises a so-called *ittiba'* – literally 'following'. *Ittiba'* means accepting every religious decision of recognised scholars and then adopting such judgments after carrying out a critical observation of the *dalil,* or scriptural evidence from the Qur'an and the Hadith (see Adams 1933).

Before embarking on to a full understanding of the Tasawuf Bahr ul-Nur, say the traditionalists, the *ana'guru,* or students from among the Sayyid and the Jawi must have passed a series of basic prerequisites set up by the teacher, the *anrongguru*; as one *ana'guru* told me:

> We must adhere faithfully by offering something in exchange for the religious lessons given by an *anrongguru*. It is these duties which prove an *ana'guru's* loyalty. When these duties are not properly met, an *ana'guru* is considered to be a traitor to his *anrongguru* and is not entitled to obtain further teachings, which in turn disvalues him even in his worldly life.

The reason for such discipline is that the Tarekat Bahr ul-Nur is the core and the most difficult module in the teachings of the Madhhab Ahl ul-Bait. The doctrines of the Madhhab Ahl ul-Bait are not formally provided in any specific place of study, unlike a common school of today in which academic

---

9   *Ahl ul-Bait*, the members of the Prophet's house comprise the five persons of his immediate family: Muhammad, Fatimah, Ali, Hasan and Husein. By extension, it embraces all descendants of these (the Sayyid). See Nurdin et al. 1977/1978, op. cit.; and Hisyam 1985, op. cit.

activities run systematically and are based on a clearly defined curriculum. Rather, the *ana'guru* must make their way to the residence of their *anrongguru*, wherever they might live. Long ago, instruction might also have taken place in traditional colleges, which the Dutch closed down during the colonial period for fear of them threatening their presence in the region. In modern Cikoang the teaching process is still run informally, sometimes secretly, though there has been a recent attempt to re-establish formal institutions, as we shall see further below.

As this study points out, the most obvious occasion of traditional visitation is that of the Maudu' festival, when *ana'guru* from all parts of Indonesia gather collectively in the house of their *anrongguru* from the 10th of the month of Safar to the 10th day of Rabi'ul Awwal of the Islamic calendar. This is the month of preparation for the Maudu' festival, Bulang Pannyongko (see Nurdin et al. 1977/1978; cf. Hisyam 1985: 59 and see Chapter Five below).

Progress in understanding along the path of the *tarekat* depends on how frequently an *ana'guru* visits the *anrongguru*; the more frequent the visits the more advanced the comprehension of the body of doctrine. In addition to this, the *anrongguru* are considered to be the best people to take charge of every religious practice conducted by their *ana'guru*, such as in the celebration of marriage, of Maudu' and of funeral rites. It is through this kind of relationship that the process of teaching and studying takes place; for example, on one occasion in a series of interviews with Sayyid Maluddin Daeng Sikki (Karaeng Sikki), a family of *ana'guru* came to visit Karaeng Sikki, their *anrongguru*, to consult upon the best day for their daughter's betrothal ceremony. The process of this consultation continued until the very last days of the wedding festivities of the family's daughter.

The relationship between *ana'guru* and *anrongguru* is very paternalistic, creating an almost fanatical loyalty among the *ana'guru* towards their master. Thus, an *ana'guru* may defer to a particular *anrongguru* only and not to others, because the '*anrongguruship*' is seen as individual and bound by religious devotion. According to one informant, the '*anrongguruship*' is not an inherited rank; rather, it is attained through the experience of the learning and teaching process. In reverse, failure to progress in the learning process is considered a possibility for all *ana'guru*, even for the children of the *anrongguru* himself.[10]

10　In reality it is only boys who are entitled to obtain religious lessons in Cikoang tradition. As one Syarifah told me, the daughters have to obtain their knowledge of religion within the family or from outside educations institutions.

In my research I chose Karaeng Sikki, chair of the al-'Aidid Organisation of Makassar as the *anrongguru* from whom I obtained the basic principles of the teachings of the Madhhab Ahl ul-Bait. The doctrines of Islamic knowledge among the Sayyid solidified around three elements to form a supposedly indivisible entity (compare Nurdin et al. 1977/1978). They are 1) *fiqh* (jurisprudence) as set out in the book of *ash-Sirat al-Mustaqim* (*The Straight Path*) from which the students were taught about *assare'a,* Islamic law and its applications; 2) *ushul al-din* (theology) relating to the *Sharaf ul-Anam* (A Story of Maulid), *Akhbar al-Akhirah* (*News of the Hereafter*) and *Aqidat ul-'Awam* (*A Beginners' Guide to Faith*) written in the Arabic alphabet, but put into in the Makassarese language by Sheikh Nur ul-din Ibnu Aly Azzanjy al-Raniri in 1634; and 3) *tasawuf* (mysticism) set out in a book called *Sharab al-'Ashikin* (*Imbibements of the Seekers*) written by Hamzah Fansuri of North Sumatra.[11]

In the third stage the students are trained in *attareka'* (Mak; In. *tarekat*) or the Sufi disciplines of *hakikah* (the final destination of obedience), *ibadah,* in which the students perform certain rituals and *zikir,* the remembrance of God by chanting names of Allah (In. *asma-asma Allah*). The main objective is to develop the *bathin,* or inward realm of the soul, which then results in *ma'rifat* (gnosis), *musyahadah* (testimony), *mukasyafah* and *mahabbah* (the loving of Allah). At the completion of this stage, the imparting of discourse on esoteric matters related to the creation of the universe and the figure of the Prophet Muhammad marks the mastery of the preceding steps. Those successful in all stages are entitled to become an *anrongguru* and to be honoured as such in their community. Their numbers may include Jawi as well as Sayyid.[12]

The traditionalists of Cikoang believe in the creation of the universe from a Bahr ul-Nur, a Sea of Light, which is also identified as the Nur Muhammad, the Divine Light of Muhammad. The Nur Muhammad is equally the beginning of the creation of all living things (see further Chapter Five). Following on from this, the Tarekat Bahr ul-Nur directs itself toward the cosmological relation between the Prophet Muhammad and Allah, with the theosophical goal of understanding the true essence of the Prophet and the final assumption that Allah as Creator and Muhammad are essentially one (see Hisyam 1985).

The belief in the cosmological pre-existence of Muhammad before his actual physical birth was first interpreted by Sahl al-Tustari, an Iraqi Sufi (d. 896 CE), and subsequently developed by his student, al-Hallaj, and other Sufi scholars

---

11   On the latter two writers see Kreemer (1922–1923) *Atjeh*, 2 vols. Leiden: E.J. Brill; cf. Bowen 1993: 44.
12   The number of Jawi, however, who become *anrongguru* is relatively small and their students tend to be drawn from fellow Jawi. No certification used to be given on the completion of studies; however I observed that there was a growing concern among the Sayyid to produce their doctrines in written form, to be distributed to all Sayyid families. Such documents have provided my main reference in the discussion of traditionalist orientations.

and writers and systematically postulated by the Sufi scholar Ibn 'Arabi. It was later to penetrate the teachings of *tasawuf* in the Muslim world. Ibn 'Arabi was most responsible for the emphasis on the role of the divine light (see Schimmel 1985). His concepts increasingly became the basis of poetic statements of Islamic piety, in which Muhammad is described as the highest-ranking man on earth, the *insan al-kamil*.

This same concept has come to underpin the social hierarchy maintained among the traditionalists of Cikoang: the Sayyid, as religious specialists, are descended from the Prophet Muhammad, himself originally of Nur Muhammad, whereas the Jawi originated from the Prophet Adam, who was created from the Nur Muhammad. This view is given a more general encryption in the phrase *'Muhamma' manggena nyawaya, Adam manggena tubuwwa'* ('Muhammad is the source of spirits, *aba ul-arwah*, while Adam is the source of bodies, *aba ul-basyar'*) (cf. Hisyam 1985: 23). Within *tasawuf*, *al-arwah*, the inward realm of *bathin*, is also given more value than *al-basyar*, or the outward realm of *lahir*.

The clear implications of the Tarekat Bahr ul-Nur are that honour is to be accorded to the Sayyid as both religious specialists and as descendants of the Prophet. This then forms the basis of all social relationships between the Sayyid and Jawi people; there is an interdependent relation between the *ana'guru* (who are mostly the Jawi, along with children of the Sayyid) and the *anrongguru* as teachers drawn from the Sayyid and a very small number of the Jawi. The pursuit of traditionalist religious, ritual and cosmological teachings still lies in the hands of the Sayyid.

The field notes which I obtained on this subject were directly completed by the Sayyid themselves, which then enabled me to come to the understanding of why the Maudu' festival is considered to be the main pillar of Islamic law and is particularly meaningful for traditionalists (see further Chapter Five).[13]

Muhammadiyah: The modernist movement

Within South Sulawesi at large, the region which takes in Cikoang, the practice of *tasawuf* was historically more popular than the study of Syari'at or Islamic law (see Safwan and Kutoyo 1981). The popularity of *tasawuf*, although essentially concerned with the belief in the oneness of God, is believed by many observers

---

13   I personally thank Sayyid Maluddin Daeng Sikki for providing all literature derived from the manuscripts and I am indebted to other traditionalist scholars: Ir. H. Najamuddin Harun al-'Aidid, Abdullah Syahran al-'Aidid, Syakhirul Najamuddin al-'Aidid and Tuan Hasan al-'Aidid, who informed me on the key concepts of the Tarekat Bahr ul-Nur.

to be accounted for as a remnant of the pre-Islamic religion of the local people. This critical point was later taken up by the modernists along the following lines.

Before Islam was adopted, the Bugis-Makassar people believed in One God called Dewata Seuwae in Bugis and Karaeng Kaminang Kammaya in Makassarese (see Chapter Two). Following the successful efforts of Datok ri Bandang (one of the three proselytising Datok) to introduce the concept of Islamic *tauhid* or monotheism, the Bugis-Makassar people began to embrace Islam. The formerly local term *pangngissengang* (inner or spiritual power) was turned to Islamic use, both culturally and terminologically, so that it is commonly known in *tasawuf* as *ilmu laduni*. At present, the process of studying *tasawuf* still incorporates many local usages, such as the gaining of invulnerability against lethal weapons, fire and so forth under the guidance of a charismatic *anrongguru*.

Such mystical phenomena continued uninterrupted until approximately the first years of the 20th century. During the last years of the 19th century, according to the historical research done by the Department of Education of Indonesia (1980–1981), the Muslims of Makassar had little formal knowledge about their religion. Islam was ascriptive in nature. The children became Muslims because their parents were Muslims. There was little effort to study the complete teachings of Islam in any ordered way.

In the first half of the 20th century, however, a larger number of religious teachers made the great pilgrimage to Mecca and returned from studying there. They brought home not only the title *al-Hajj* or *Haji*, but also the inspiration of the writings of the founding fathers of the modernist-reformist movement, the peripatetic Jamaluddin al-Afghani (1839–1897) and Muhammad Abduh (1849–1905), a famous *ulama* in Egypt, as well as the influence of the strict revivalist Saudi Wahhabi movement at Mecca. These returning religious scholars then influenced the religious orientation of the Makassarese.

Echoes of modernist thinking became more clearly heard in Makassar after the official founding of a branch of the organisation of Muhammadiyah (Followers of Muhammad) in the region on 4 April 1926, only five years after Kiyai Haji Muhammad Dahlan founded the central structure in Yogyakarta on 18 November 1912. The first chairperson of the branch in Ujung Pandang, with its 17 members, was Haji Yusuf Daeng Mattiro. This organisation adopted the methods of modern management in running the educational institutions, which it then set up. Its main aim was to purify the Islamic faith of local 'variations' and to turn the non-Islamic elements still existing in such practices to the central tenets of the Qur'an and Hadith. In general studies of Indonesian Muslims, the Muhammadiyah is seen as the reform movement that most strongly objected to mystical practices and targeted the *tarekat* (see Shihab 1995).

The strength of the Muhammadiyah lay in its system of schools. The educational institutions it provided in Ujung Pandang were initially run informally as *pengajian,* or religious study sessions, and were conducted circulating from private home to home. When a young *ulama* from Minangkabau named Haji Abdul Malik Karim Amrullah, more commonly known as HAMKA, came to Ujung Pandang, he saw that the *pengajian* needed to be institutionalised. The result of his proposal was that in 1932 a *sekolah tabligh,* or missionary school, was founded and soon changed to Muallimin Muhammadiyah (Muhammadiyah Schooling) in 1934.

Once this school took shape, local Makassar Muslims became familiar with the use of classrooms, writing boards and classes run through regular programs. The teachers came mostly from the Minangkabau region of West Sumatra and cities such as its capital Padang. Their students were instructed in preparation to become Islamic teachers and missionaries, *muballigh,* and on graduating were placed within the region of South Sulawesi. On October 1945, during the revolutionary era of the struggle for national independence, a Perguruan Islam Datumuseng (Datumuseng Islamic Institution) was set up. Among its founding fathers were Haji Mansyur Daeng Tompo, Haji Gazali Syachlan, Haji Darwis Zakariah, Haji Muhiddin Daeng Sikki, Luthan Muhammad and others. The reformist organisation of Persis (In. Persatuan Islam; Muslim Unity) set up in Bandung in 1923 also offered its assistance. The Datumuseng institution was founded upon two motivations: first, to show opposition to the invaders, Japan, who had closed down several institutions owned by Muhammadiyah under their tight censorship, and the second was to encourage all Muslims to join the fight against colonialism.

After Indonesia gained its independence in 1945, the primary objectives of Perguruan Islam Datumuseng and Muhammadiyah were to find ways to purify the faith of local Muslims. In reality, many Muslims *were* keen practitioners of Islam: they performed the five daily prayers, attended the Friday congregations (Ar. *jum'ah*), fasted during the holy month of Ramadhan and displayed a real piety, but at the same time they took part in pre-Islamic ceremonials, such as making offerings to sacred places or objects. Many still believed in the reality of the pre-Islamic God. As another example, they regularly visited sacred tombs and brought offerings, not for the sake of the souls of the deceased, but to ask for prosperity, health and other good fortune. So the Makassar Muslims tended to meet their Islamic duties while still participating in local customs (In. *adat*; Mak. *ada* and Bug. *ade*).[14]

---

14   The most popular tomb visited in Gowa and in Makassar as a whole is that of Syekh Yusuf, known as Ko'banga. He was one of the most outspoken teachers against local practices at the height of the kingdom of Gowa. Interestingly, in contemporary Gowa the local people visit his tomb for exactly the same purposes.

In regard to their religious beliefs, the Makassar Muslims of South Sulawesi, particularly those in the rural areas, were always mindful that the Qur'an and the Hadith were the sources of their religious doctrines and duties. They were the centres of their faith, which all good Muslims must try to observe and apply in their daily activities. Almost all traditionalists are able to recite some Arabic texts relevant to their needs. Since childhood, many had been familiar with the reading of the Qur'an aloud, even though they did not know the literal meaning or the proper application of the texts. In their religious practices they preferred to recite, instead of the Qur'an, the Barazanji, or the special Arabic prayers offered on the birth of the Prophet. These were also used on various occasions such as at the celebration of weddings, the Maudu' festival and for Pattumateang, or ritual purification. At other times, a more Islamic part was simply added on to an otherwise almost completely traditional ritual. This became the main issue leading to the dispute between the Muhammadiyah and the local traditionalist Muslims in modern Ujung Pandang and South Sulawesi at large.

Within the religious environment of Cikoang, as is freely admitted by the modernists, it has been difficult to make inroads. The Muhammadiyah was never able to found a sub-branch, in the face of strong opposition by the local people. When asked about this, an informant told me, 'It is impossible to found a Muhammadiyah sub-branch in this region (Kampong Cikoang), because all Muslims here are adherents of the traditionalist organisation NU (Nahdhatul Ulama; Revival of Religious Scholars) – not organisationally, but practically.' Another informant told me that there was a Muhammadiyah sub-branch located in another village called Lengkese, in the same district as Cikoang. Yet, as he went on:

> The majority of its members derive from outside regions, because none of the local people are brave enough to become members. Even the chairperson of the Muhammadiyah sub-branch, Daeng Sila asked my grandfather, who was a Sayyid, to lead the funeral rituals for his father. This was because he showed respect more to my grandfather than to other non-Sayyid religious specialists.

So for the local people the Muhammadiyah, as an institution, is seen as an outsider group intolerant of their traditions, whereas the Sayyid are still held to be the religious specialists on whom they are emotionally and intellectually dependent. The following cases illustrate such phenomena, as told by my informants in Jakarta.

Case 1. Time: Unrecorded

> One day a Muhammadiyah lecturer delivered a religious talk (In. *ceramah agama*) in a mosque in Cikoang. He was immediately asked by the congregation (In. *jama'ah*) to leave the mosque and never to come to Cikoang again if he still wanted to live, because he had offended the local people by criticising the Maudu' festival.

After this incident, no members of Muhammadiyah ever again tried to approach Cikoang for the purpose of preaching their doctrines. It is on the recommendations of the local people that the authorities have not allowed the organisation to found a sub-branch in the region. Yet the Sayyid residing outside Cikoang but forming their own exclusive community also face a number of problems in maintaining their long-standing religious practices.

Many Sayyid in Jakarta narrate the following two events which occurred in Ujung Pandang over their relatives' conflict with those who supported Muhammadiyah.

Case 2. Time: Late 1970s

> A Sayyid Karaeng named Karaeng Sarro, living in Banta-Bantaeng, Ujung Pandang near the mosque of emigrant Muhajirin had an argument with a member of Muhammadiyah who also lived in the region. The conflict arose when that person criticised the Maudu' festival while delivering a *khotbah*, or Friday sermon, in the mosque. Upon hearing it, Karaeng Sarro immediately stood up and told that person never to criticise the Maudu' festival unless he wanted to put himself at risk. Karaeng Sarro continued that a religious talk should give people happiness and coolness and not the reverse of a feeling of offence. The conflict was not yet over, because Karaeng Sarro asked several of his relatives in Cikoang to help him patrol that person's house for a number of weeks.

This is only one among many similar cases experienced by Sayyid living outside Cikoang. It indicates the strong fanaticism of the Sayyid in countering outside criticism of their religious traditions.

The case below also interestingly demonstrates the attempt of one Sayyid who challenged his own Sayyid traditions.

Case 3. Time: Unrecorded

> A Sayyid graduating from IAIN (Institut Agama Islam Negeri; State Islamic Institute) in Ujung Pandang who supported the modernist movement used to be keen to challenge the religious orientation of his Sayyid relatives, notably regarding *kafa'ah,* Maudu' and Pattumateang. Facing strong resistance from his relatives he then had to move to another city, Palu (the capital of the province of Central Sulawesi), to save his life and that of his family. After several years his wife divorced him and he became an object of ridicule by his Sayyid relatives. One Sayyid then reconfirmed the danger of challenging the long-standing traditions of the Sayyid.
>
> Yet this does not mean that once the Cikoangese (particularly the Sayyid) have studied at the IAIN or similar modernist schools they will automatically support the modernist movement. Cases like the above are, I think, rare and not a general reflection of all Cikoangese. I found a Sayyid Tuan who is a graduate of a typical *pesantren,* or religious boarding school of the modernists, and he remains proud of his Sayyid traditions. He told me, 'We are well prepared to critically accept what we are learning at school. If my teacher criticises the Maudu' festival, I will then think that he or she does not understand its significance for the Cikoangese. So it is just easy not to be influenced.'

The many cases exemplified by the above have forced the Muhammadiyah to be more cautious in its religious mission. Pak Syamsuddin, a non-Cikoangese from Makassar who has experienced the fanaticism of the Sayyid, and is the chief director of the Muhammadiyah branch in Luar Batang hamlet, Northern Jakarta, said:

> We tend not to use a Muhammadiyah 'cloth' (the Muhammadiyah label) when approaching the Cikoangese, because it has become the most hated word for them. We participate in their ritual practices, as individuals, in order to show our solidarity. If I am asked to deliver a speech, I never mention any of the Muhammadiyah doctrines. Since we have practised that method over the last ten years, we have been trusted to become the religious instructors (In. *guru mengaji*) of their children. We are now considered to be as capable as their own religious specialists (the Sayyid) and we hope that we can teach the younger generations about the basic teachings of Islam.

He then recounted a number of ceremonies conducted by the Sayyid to which he was invited as a guest. This method is applied generally in educational institutions of the Muhammadiyah organisation. Students are being taught how to construct a bridge between a complete implementation of Islamic law and the students' previous beliefs about Islam (Shihab 1995). In other words, the

Muhammadiyah is trying to approach the local Muslims by a gentle means and at the same time is searching for compromise solutions. I interviewed a student from a Cikoangese family named Nurdin. He said:

> After studying here (with the Muhammadiyah) I became more acquainted with the teachings of my religion. For example, I had known how to recite *Surah al-Ikhlas* (one of the shortest chapters in the Qur'an emphasising the oneness of God) since I was a little kid, but I never knew its location in the Qur'an and its proper meaning until I became a student there.

And after realising the benefit of studying at Muhammadiyah schools he registered his own children in their educational institutions.

Within the arguments around religious life in Cikoang, the modernists have given both oral and written explanations of their position, most of them advocating that the beliefs and practices of the traditionalists be purified. Their reasoning is quite clear: although the traditionalists regard themselves as being adherents to Sunnism, in the Maudu' festival especially they embrace an exaggerated version of the Prophet Muhammad as somehow supernatural. In order to show their love and admiration for him, the traditionalists see his character imbued in the actual material objects used in the composition of the rituals. The modernists, however, have learned not to impose their expectations on such elements of the traditionalist practices, which they do otherwise criticise. Rather, they must attempt to find other personal ways to bridge the gap between themselves and the traditionalists.

CHAPTER FIVE

The Festivals of Maudu' and Pattumateang

This chapter describes in detail the celebration of the festivals of Maudu' and Pattumateang from the perspective of the traditionalist Muslims of Cikoang and explores elements of both to which the modernists raise their objections. While there is some participation in the ceremonies by the modernists, I discuss the extent to which the two groups differ in their performance. Each of the parties justifies its own practice with reference to the same sources, while remaining different in spirit and application.

Maudu': Celebrating the birth of the Prophet

Maulid or Maulud (from the Arabic root meaning 'birth') is a holiday occurring on the 12th day of the month of Rabi'ul Awwal of the Islamic calendar to commemorate the Prophet Muhammad's birth. It is a yearly festival celebrated in many Muslim regions, with religious gatherings associated with feasting and the reciting of *barazanji*, or special prayers praising events in the life of Muhammad.[1]

---

[1] The Arabic source book of Barzanji tells the legends of the Prophet, collected and edited by Ja'afar ibn Hasan al-Barzanji (d. 1766, Medina), a *qadi*, or judge, of the Maliki law school. The ceremonial recitation is known in the Makassarese context as *a'rate'*. See Carl Brockelmann 1898–1902, 1937–1942. Z: 384, S2: 517; Knappert 1961: 24–31; also see Schimmel 1985 on the Maulid.

For the Muslims of Cikoang, Maulid, locally more commonly called Maudu', is a feast day.² It is said to have first been conducted in the region on 8 Rabi'ul Awwal 1041 AH (1620 CE) on the initiative of Sayyid Jalaluddin and I-Bunrang and was performed in I-Bunrang's house. On that occasion Sayyid Jalaluddin asked I-Bunrang's aid to provide 10 of litres of rice, 40 chickens and 120 chicken or duck eggs for 40 guests. For this first Maudu' there were 40 Kanre Maudu', or Maudu' meals, presented in bamboo baskets. In the following year, on 12 Rabi'ul Awwal 1042 AH, the number of participants had increased greatly. Every participant, representing his household, was therefore asked to prepare a Kanre Maudu'. This was known as Maudu' Ca'di (In. Maulid Kecil or Small Maulid) prepared under the guidance of an *anrongguru*. The contents of the Kanre Maudu' consist of four litres of rice, one chicken, one coconut and at least one egg for each member of the household.

From around 1050 AH the number of participants in the festival continued to increase and the Maudu' needed to be held in a larger location, later called Maudu' Lompoa (Mak.; In. Maulid Besar or Great Maulid). It is alleged that it was both Sayyid Umar and Sayyid Sahabuddin, the sons of Sayyid Jalaluddin who created the Maudu' Lompoa.

In modern Cikoang the preparation of Maudu' Ca'di remains intact as the opening program of the festival. From the 12th to the last days of Rabi'ul Awwal, all members of the al-'Aidid clan are given the opportunity to arrive in Cikoang village prior to the celebration of Maudu' Lompoa, which forms the culminating point of the whole ritual. The households preparing the Kanre Maudu' come from many different parts of Indonesia: Jakarta, Kalimantan, Sumbawa, Palu and other areas, such as Selayar, Buton, Luwu, Mandar and Kaili. Those who cannot come under constraints of time or money will donate to others making the journey. Thus the Kanre Maudu' are representative of all households involved with the celebration.

Once the *Maudu' Ca'di* is complete the *Maudu' Lompoa* begins and the households of the al-'Aidid clan gather publicly at the edge of the Cikoang river (Mak. je'ne Cikoang; In. Sungai Cikoang, see the maps on page 18 of this volume). Small boats called *julung-julung* are jammed together in pairs, in which the Kanre Maudu' are placed. The *julung-julung* are then set astride a real boat. According to my informant, the number of *julung-julung* indicates the number of marriages conducted throughout the year in the Sayyid families. The *julung-julung* are also called *bunting beru*, or 'newly married couples'. Karaeng Sikki explained to me the religious reason for using boats in the festival; he quoted the Prophet Muhammad to the effect that 'anyone who rides in the boat of the Ahl ul-Bait

---

2 Apart from my own observations, the following description draws on the book *Peringatan Maulid Nabi di Cikoang* issued by Kerukunan Keluarga Al-'Aidid and a long interview with H. Maluddin Karaeng Sikki.

(Household of the Prophet), his or her life will be pleasant in the Hereafter.' Karaeng Sikki interpreted this to refer to any couples whose marriage was based on the Sayyid marriage system of *kafa'ah*. They will remain as members of the Family of the Prophet and will have a place among the blessed.

The modernist Muslims agree with the celebration of the Maudu' festival as long as it is held for the purpose of introducing the Prophet's teachings, so that people become more acquainted with the doctrines. If such is the reason for conducting the Maudu', then it is *mubah* (Ar.) or of neutral value, neither forbidden nor prescribed in Islam. For the traditionalists, however, the Maudu' festival is the occasion for a high ritual meal of remembrance of the character of the Prophet.

Hisyam (1985) and Hamonic (1985) observed that the traditionalists of Cikoang believe that truly pious Muslims have the duty to pay respect to the Maudu' festival by celebrating it as lavishly as possible, while other religious practices, including the set five daily prayers, are accorded less priority. Another interesting point is that, for the traditionalists, participation in the Maudu' festival is regarded as having rewards equal to those of making the great pilgrimage to Mecca, the *hajj* (In. *naik haji*) which is the fifth and the last fundamental pillar of Islam. This understanding has had a wide impact on the socio-cultural development of Cikoang. Every activity of the community throughout the year is directed toward the Maudu' festival, reaching a peak between the months of Safar and Rabi'ul Awwal.

Nobody in the community will consciously go against these long-standing traditions without facing terrible obstacles. One *anrongguru* quoted a Hadith to me, saying 'Anyone who does not perform the Maudu' festival in the month of Rabi'ul Awwal, which is the month of the Prophet Muhammad's birth, will be cursed on the Qur'an and the Bible. While he or she walks on earth, they will be cursed by the earth as walking dogs and pigs.' The following local verses also strengthen this belief:

1. *Manna tena kusambayang, assalak a'maudukmamak, antama tonjarisuruga pappinyamang.*
   Though I do not perform the salat prayers, as long as I perform the Maudu', paradise will be mine.

2. *Ka'deji kunipapile, assambayang na'mauduka, kualleangang a'mauduka ri Nabbia.*
   If I am asked to choose between prayers and Maudu', I will choose Maudu' for the sake of the Prophet.

3. *Tassitaunga 'kareso, a'panassa pangngasselang, tena maraeng nakupa'maudukang ri Nabbia.*

   Every year I work hard, collecting much money, for nothing but Maudu' for the sake of the Prophet.

4. *Tepoki memang bukunnu, akkareso bangngi allo, sollanna niak sallang nupa'maudukang.*

   Let everything in our power, working hard day or night, contain something for conducting for Maudu'.

5. *I nakke kaniakkangku, I lalang ri anne lino, tena maraeng, passangali a'mauduk.*

   My existence on this earth is but nothing, if not directed to Maudu'.

6. *Manna memangja kumate, susa tena la'busu'na kuparetonji, maudu'ku ri Nabbia.*

   Even though I may lie dying, my last efforts would turn, to making my Maudu' for the Prophet.

7. *Balukangi tedonnu, pappita'gallangi tananu, nu' maudu' mamo.*

   Let buffalo be sold, let the land be pawned, for the purpose only of Maudu'.

8. *Anngaipaka nuranggaselakamma, nupattaenai baran-barannu, naiya minne paggaukang kaminang mala'biri.*

   Why do you nurse regret, on sacrificing your belongings, when this is the most honourable deed.[3]

According to my findings, this traditional belief is in fact not entirely universal among the Sayyid. It seems that among some members of the clan there are different interpretations of the significance of the Maudu' celebrations. This opposition, arising within the Sayyid community itself, is not commonplace, however. The numbers of those who have doubts about the significance of the practice are very small and what is more, the consequences of such an opposition, if expressed publicly, may bring down punishment from the wider Sayyid community, such as taunts or even killings (see Chapter Four).

So in reality, for the most part, the traditionalists' respect for the Maudu' festival runs deep. This is most apparent during the month of Rabi'ul Awwal, when no other religious practices, even due life-cycle rites, may be conducted.

---

3   Manyambeang 1984.

Bulang Pannyongko: The month of preparation

All participants of the Maudu' festival have one month in which to prepare their Kanre Maudu'. From the 10th day of Safar to the 10th of Rabi'ul Awwal, family members of the al-'Aidid clan gather, numbering 20 to 40 heads of households acting under the guidance of an *opua*, a Sayyid Karaeng. Representatives from among the household heads are then chosen to prepare Kanre Maudu' for all the family members they represent. Every family member, including children, must donate at least four litres of rice, one chicken, one coconut and one chicken or duck egg towards the making of the Kanre Maudu'.

According to my informants, during this month of preparation, the sanctity of the items must be preserved; for example, to keep them clean, the chickens must be put in a bamboo stockade for the whole month and only consume good food given by the owners, the Sayyid, until slaughter. The people in charge of the preparations must make their ablutions (Ar. *wudhu'*) – the same purification of the body with water as precedes the *salat* prayers. The women involved in the preparations must be clear from menstruation. Transgression against these rules will annul the whole preparation process (see Nurdin et al. 1977/1978). The participants should also be in a state of inner sincerity when they donate their belongings to make the Kanre Maudu', because the festival is also seen as a time of giving charity to the needy (Mak. *passidakkang*; In. *sedekah*).

Kanre Maudu': The Maudu' foods

Regarding the foodstuffs for the festival, after they are finished cooking, the ingredients of Kanre Maudu' – rice, chicken, coconuts and eggs – are placed into a number of bamboo storage baskets, locally called *bakul duduk*. The rice alone, however, must be only half-cooked (Mak. *nipamatarak*; In. *setengah matang*). It is the job of the people to whom the Kanre Maudu' are given who will cook the rice finally later on, so that it does not spoil before being consumed (see Manyambeang 1984). The chickens are fried with curry powder and placed in the *bakul duduk*. The cooked eggs are tinted with bright colours, often red, then are threaded on to a half-metre long thin stick and arranged in rows and circles on top of the *bakul duduk* (see Figure 9). The *bakul duduk* may also sometimes include sweet cookies and a selection of snacks.[4]

---

[4] For more description of the making of Kanre Maudu' in Cikoang see Nurdin et al. 1977/1978; Harmonic 1985; and compare a similar set of practices in the Gayo highlands (Bowen 1993: 237–240).

The number of *bakul duduk* are then arranged on *bembengan* (Mak.; In. *usungan*) or wooden litters. The *bembengan* is quadrangle-shaped at its base, which is topped by a frame, a *kandawari* or another similar but smaller shape called *sulapa'*. The dimensions of the *bembengan* are made in size as to whether the Kanre Maudu' is for an individual or for a family. Finally, the *bembengan* are placed into a small boat, supported by four 1-metre-long poles, called *julung-julung* (see Figure 10).

Figure 9: The *kandawari* and *sulapa'* are put in a *bembengan*

Figure 10: The *kandawari* are put on top of the *julung-julung*

In order to understand how the Maudu' festival is organised within its ritual composition, let us begin with a mystical verse quoted from traditionalist teachings: 'Allah created the light of Muhammad unequalled in beauty. The *Nur Muhammad* resembled the body hair of a peacock, and then it was poured into a crystal glass and placed in *Shajarat ul-Yaqin*, the Tree of Faith' (H. Maluddin Daeng Sikki).

As we have seen earlier, the preliminary items of Kanre Maudu' consist of a number of live chickens. These symbolise both the peacock as a symbol of beauty (Ar. *jamal*) and the mercy inherent in the Nur Muhammad. The *bakul duduk*, being made of bamboo, are white and represent the crystal glass. The towering *kandawari* stands for the Shajarat ul-Yaqin. The decorative colouring of the items of Kanre Maudu' also reflect the perfection and beauty of the Nur Muhammad. The red and white eggs are a symbol of the spirits surrounding it. The brightly coloured sails decorating the boats symbolise the banners of al-Mu'minin (the Faithful of Islam) which will safeguard believers on the Day of Judgement (Ar. Yaum ul-Masyar). Fruits and plaited and woven materials illustrate prosperity, vitality and cheerfulness, welcoming the creation of the divine light of Muhammad and the creation of the whole universe. Thus, the celebration of the Maulid/Maudu' festival in Cikoang can be seen as a visual representation of the creation of Nur Muhammad and the Prophet Muhammad before his earthly existence.

In the course of the festival, the Kanre Maudu' are grouped and brought to the site of celebration at the edge of the Cikoang river (see maps on page 18 of this volume). This event is called 'the procession of the Kanre Maudu' (*anngantara kanre maudu'*) Now the Maudu' Lompoa of the Great Maudu' proper begins, when the *julung-julung* are set in place on the riverbank. At the Maudu' Lompoa held in 1996, there were 15 *julung-julung* in all, indicating that there were 15 *bunting beru*, or newly married couples, whose weddings had been conducted in the preceding year.

A'rate: Reciting the Barazanji

Once all the *julung-julung* have been assembled by the riverbank of *je'ne Cikoang*, the largest of them is chosen as a stage for the recitation of the Barazanji (Mak. A'rate'). Tens of *parate'*, or readers, seat themselves with crossed legs. Then for more than two hours the *parate'* recite the Barazanji, singly by turns and then in chorus. The Barazanji, also locally termed *jikkiri* or *zikir* from the terminology of Sufism, contain stories of the life of the Prophet Muhammad, re-modified, according to tradition, by Sayyid Jalaluddin himself (see Nurdin et al. 1977/1978; cf. Hamonic 1985).

Before the singing gets under way, all the owners of the Kanre Maudu' have been summoned to see the collection of the feasts. There are amusing moments as each owner exaggerates how fine his offering is and disparages those of other people. This occasion is called *a'ganda*, meaning 'multiplication', 'increment', or even 'exaggeration' (see Nurdin et al. 1977/1978). Arguments erupt over whose Kanre Maudu' is the best, which sometimes leads to mock physical fights, and each participant strives to plunge his enemy under the water of the Cikoang River. After this the participants change out of their wet clothes and return to join the ensuing programs without any hard feelings. After the A'rate the gatherings recite Shalawat, or blessings upon the Prophet and his family, as well as his close companions.

Pa'bageang Kanre Maudu': Distributing the food baskets

After reciting the Shalawat, all the guests invited by the Sayyid community — prominent intellectuals, heads of religious institutions from outside Cikoang, heads of surrounding villages, heads of districts and other distinguished people, along with all the participants — are served meals and drinks, which are not taken from the Kanre Maudu' but provided specially for the guests.

This stage is called the *pattoanang*, or reception. Then the Kanre Maudu' are distributed by the head Sayyid Karaeng of the festival in ordered stages – not to the participants, which is unlawful – but to a number of selected figures of prominence. This is called *pa'bageang* Kanre Maudu'.

First, the Qadhi', Islamic judges and the *imam*, the leaders of the communal prayers who are not from among the Sayyid community are presented with the Kanre Maudu' as gifts. The second group in the hierarchy of distribution are the parate' and the heads of nearby villages and heads of districts. Finally, the rest of the Kanre Maudu' are distributed to the crowd, mostly the poor. Lengths of fabric and unsown sarongs decorating the *julung-julung* also used to be distributed in the past, but are now collected and sold by the head of Mangarabombang district for financing the development of Kampong Cikoang (see Nurdin et al. 1977/1978). Therewith, all stages of the Maudu' festival are complete.

The modernists, debating the validity of Maudu', object to its interpretation as a ritual meal and an obligatory practice (cf. Bowen 1993). For them, its celebration was never commanded by Allah nor recommended by the Prophet Muhammad himself. According to one modernist scholar, the first Maulid festival was held by Sultan Salahuddin al-'Ayyub in 1187 CE, more than 500 years after the death of the Prophet, and was done for the purpose of raising the spirits of the Muslim soldiers fighting in the Crusades.

Popular commemorations of Maulid in Ujung Pandang and Jakarta, where most modernists reside, take the form of didactic lectures at which an *ulama*, or scholar, recounts the magnificence of the life of the Prophet from the time of his childhood as an orphan up to the events of his prophetic mission. These are held for the purpose of introducing the Prophet's teachings, so that people will become more acquainted with and remember the doctrine. Haji Malik, one of the most outspoken modernist scholars in Ujung Pandang, tends to stress the role of the Prophet Muhammad as an exemplary human figure. He and others believe that 'if the inclusion of any meal in the celebration is intended to be offered to the spirit of the Prophet, or even to represent his physical self, then it is *bid'ah*, a heretical and forbidden innovation.' This statement should be set against a real life event, as one Sayyid told me:

> In the Maudu' festival of 1996, there was invited a Muhammadiyah Imam living in Ujung Pandang. When the Kanre Maudu' was distributed to him, he received it happily, he even took the biggest one. We sometimes laughed when we remembered that occasion, because we knew that Muhammadiyah members criticised the inclusion of food in the Maudu' festival, but they ate it when we gave it. That is hypocritical.

Opposed ideas about a proper way of conducting the Maudu' festival between modernist and traditionalist scholars rarely come into the public sphere, however. The modernists take part in the celebrations, but only as guests. This is not because they are not allowed to participate but, as was mentioned to me by one modernist, this is the most tactful way to show their disagreement.

Pattumateang: Purifying the deceased

According to the traditionalists, death is a matter entirely in the hands of Allah. It is one of the divine signs of God (In. *tanda-tanda kekuasaan Allah*), which no human being can predict.[5] When its time comes, the only thing humans should do is to submit. Moreover, for the *anrongguru*, the religious specialists of the traditionalists, death is not the end but the passage into the next and eternal existence. It is yet another realm for humans to enter, called *alam barzakh*, a purgatorial period between death and Judgment Day, before entering the hereafter (Ar. *al-akhirat*; In. *alam akhirat*). The modernists agree with this doctrine. Pak Syamsuddin recited the verse of the Qur'an (QS 3: 185) which proclaims that 'every soul will experience death'.

According to the traditionalist point of view, death entails a further process of human interaction through which the dead are assisted by the living. Pattumateang, literally 'purifying the deceased' conducted after the burial service, is a means through which the living can transfer merit to the dead. Modernists object to this latter assumption by asking: 'How can the dead be responsive to what the living are trying to do for them?' The traditionalist argument is to do with proper practice and the salvationist intent behind it. They ask in return: 'What are the living supposed to do for the dead? What is the purpose of performing a particular rite for the dead?' (Compare Bowen 1993: 251.)

On a November day in 1996,[6] in Tuan Kebo's house in the centre of the hamlet of Luar Batang, I met with a Makassar man named Pak Kadir, who excused himself from my interviewing to go and attend the Pattumateang of a Sayyid *anrongguru* who had died three days before. Before leaving, Pak Kadir accompanied me for a while to visit one Tuan Ridwan, who recounted the last conversation between him and the deceased Sayyid. Tuan Ridwan told me: 'Several days before that Sayyid died, I was told that I must prepare for his Pattumateang soon because he was to die in two days. After two days, death really did come to him. Is it

---

5   The others are birth (In. *kelahiran*), livelihood (In. *rezki*) and marriage partner (In. *jodoh*).
6   This account is taken directly from my field notes. It was Pak Kadir, Tuan Kebo's guest, who became one of my key informants during my stay in Jakarta and who introduced me to other Sayyid living in the district.

a coincidence? No, it is not, because I have previously experienced this kind of matter twice.' My Sayyid informant repeatedly said that death should not be sorrowful. Rather, it must be accepted as a natural disposition of humankind. What the living should do is to help the deceased pass to the *alam barzakh* peacefully, that is, by performing the ritual of Pattumateang.[7]

Pattumateang, or Attumate (Mak.), the purification of the departed, is conducted day and night for 40 days from the third night after the burial service. In the traditionalist perspective, the soul of the deceased will step over seven points of crossing, or cross-examination, all taking place at night in the 40-day-long journey, before it is entitled to enter paradise (see below). This cross-examination is locally called Bahrullah, from the Arabic for the 'Sea of Allah.'

The first crossing is on the third night, the second crossing is on the seventh night, the third crossing is on the 10th night, the fourth crossing is on the 15th night, the fifth crossing is on the 20th night, the sixth crossing is on the 30th and the seventh crossing is on the 40th night. The 40th and last night is said to be the point of determination as to whether the soul is to enter paradise or hell. Pattumateang is therefore compulsory because it is a means to help release the deceased soul smoothly through the crossing (see Manyambeang 1984).

There are elements in the Pattumateang practice to be performed by the family of the deceased, led by the deceased's *anrongguru* during life; these are *assurommacakanre sibokoi* and *appanaung panganreang segang katinroang*.

Assurommacakanre sibokoi: Recitations over the food

On the third night after the burial service, which is the deceased's first journey in the *bahrullah*, the *anrongguru* guides the gatherings in the collective recitation of Shalawat and Taslim, phrases meaning 'Peace be upon Him' (the Prophet) as follows:

Allahumma shalli 'ala sayyidina Muhammadin nabi al-ummi wa 'ala alihi wa ashabihi wa salam.

God, call down blessings on our master Muhammad the unlettered prophet and on His family and companions, and greet them with peace.

---

7 Pak Kadir observed that there is a clear distinction between the Pattumateang held for the Sayyid and Karaeng and that conducted for ordinary Makassarese. If the deceased is Sayyid or Karaeng the body will be laid out, in state, as it were, in the front living room, the best room in the house, whereas if the deceased belongs to the lower orders the body will be placed in any of the rooms.

At the time of death agony, people in Cikoang will have recited the *talqing* (Mak.; Ar. *talqin*) a catechism intended to remind the dying person about the primary tenets of Islam and to help release the departing soul to be smoothly taken away by Malakul maut, the angel of death. According to the traditionalists, there will be two other angels, Mungkar and Nakir, whose task is to interrogate the deceased's soul in the *alam barzakh*. Dead Sayyid have nothing to worry about, say the traditionalists, because the two angels are also Sayyid.[8]

This occasion, called *assuromacakanre sibokoi*, means 'asking the living to recite over food for the deceased'. The traditionalists believe the recitation of Shalawat and Taslim are necessary in order to inform the Prophet Muhammad that one of his family, a member of the Ahl al-Bait has died. The gathering also collectively chants the Qur'an, known locally as *attadarusu* (Mak.; In. *tadarusan*) and more particularly the *Akhbar ul-Akhirah* (*News of the Hereafter*), a book telling the progress of the deceased from the time life is taken away to the journey to paradise. According to the traditionalists, the recitation of the *Akhbar ul-Akhirah* will help the soul of the deceased in successfully finding its way and it will not get lost. Throughout the 40 days and nights of this continuing ritual, the participants are served meals of food and drink by their hosts, the family of the deceased.

On the 40th and last night, the host must offer a sacrificed animal to become the deceased's 'vehicle' on its way through the seven crossings. The type of animal given is based on the level of the deceased's rank in society. If the deceased is from among the Sayyid Karaeng, his or her family must slaughter at least one buffalo, the most expensive sacrificial animal in the region. Nevertheless, this is only valid in normal situations. A chicken or a goat is acceptable when the family cannot afford a buffalo. A poor Sayyid Karaeng is allowed to have only a chicken sacrificed for him. The Sayyid do not, however, always match their economic capacities with rank or status levels in this matter.

So the traditionalists believe that the Pattumateang and the feasting assist the soul of the deceased to erase sins and to make the journey to paradise. The modernists, by contrast, object to the salvationist intention behind the reading of the Qur'an and so forth and the inclusion of food in the rituals. Pak Syamsuddin, for example, maintained 'it is *bid'ah* and pointless, if one intends to present the Qur'an verses recited for the sake of the dead'. He argued that no other person can erase the sins of the dead; it is only the dead who can be responsible for their own behaviour in life.

---

8   On the role of these two angels, see for Egypt, Lane 1860: 522–25; for Morocco, Westermarck 1926, II: 464–65; and cf. Bowen 1993: 255.

Popular ceremonies after the burial service conducted in Ujung Pandang and Jakarta are called *ta'ziah* (Ar.; 'times of remembering notions of death'). *Ta'ziah*, which are held for three to six nights, comprise a series of face-to-face lectures in which an *ulama* delivers religious talks (In. *ceramah agama*) encouraging all humankind to be in a state of preparation for death. At one of the *ta'ziah* I attended the *ulama* said; 'we, the living, during our lifetime should not waste time in pursuit of worldly things, because when death comes to us, the only thing we bring with us to face Allah is the account of our good deeds. So before death we should concentrate on good deeds (e.g. by helping the needy) as much as we can.'

During the *ta'ziah*, the hosts also often serve guests with food and drink. This is another cause for objection by the modernists, because according to Pak Syamsuddin, 'If the host provides food and drinks, that makes it a meal party and this is what Islam does not accept, because it will double the disadvantage of the deceased in the *alam barzakh*'. Bowen (1993) found that among the Gayo of Sulawesi that the consumption of food in the house of the dead is considered tantamount to corrupting away the food of orphans – meaning that the sins of this action will flow on to the dead.

Appanaung panganreang segang katinroang: Bringing down delicacies with a bed

This comprises the last section of the Pattumateang, where all the participants, particularly those in charge of reciting Shalawat and Taslim, the Qur'an and *Akhbar ul-Akhirah* are given gifts in appreciation of their 40 days of attendance at the Pattumateang. The *anrongguru* receives the largest gift, because he will have played the most important role in the proceedings.

This occasion is called *appanaung panganreang segang katinroang* – meaning 'the offering of favourite food and that of the bed' – the bed stands for that which the deceased liked most during their lifetime, and is offered to the former *anrongguru*. The 'food' consists of a large cupboard containing food, cakes and desserts, while the 'bed' or household wherewithal is sometimes a new one, or at least the former bed of the deceased, together with its linen and pillows. All are presented to the deceased's *anrongguru*. This custom provides yet another cause for opposition by the modernists, on the reasoning that the awarding of gifts to the *anrongguru* is not necessary, especially if it comes at the expense of the grieving family of the deceased.

The arguments adduced by the modernists are based on the teachings of Imam Shafi'i, the founder of the Sunni Shafi'i school of law, with reference to a Hadith which says: 'If a child of Adam (a human being) dies, all but three of his or her good deeds are held above reckoning: charity given during his or her lifetime, applied knowledge and a pious child to pray for his or her sake.' One of my modernist informants, Pak Syamsuddin, said that if the deceased in his or her lifetime has made a donation, to the building of mosque, for example, the reward of that deed will continuously flow to the spirit of the deceased whenever the mosque is used for prayer or other religious activities. If pious children of the deceased recite prayers for the sake of their dead parents, God will unquestionably answer their prayers. Nevertheless, Pak Syamsuddin added, children cannot not erase the sins of their dead parents. The most they can do is ask God for His mercy.

It is these same three good deeds of one's lifetime, said the modernists – charity, useful knowledge and pious children who continue to pray for their dead parents – that will sustain the well-being of the deceased in *alam barzakh*. It is not sustained through the reciting of verses of the Qur'an under the guidance of the deceased's former *anrongguru*, nor the slaughter of a sacrificial animal for serving to the guests in the 40th night of the Pattumateang. Pak Syamsuddin then went on to criticise the expense borne by the family for the feasting:

> It is supposed to be the remaining family members who are entitled to receive food from the guests, not the reverse. They are in mourning, they need both moral and material aid. How can one ask for food from those who are in need of help? It is corrupting.

On another occasion Pak Syamsuddin narrated to me his experience when he was invited as a guest to Pattumateang proceedings:

> When the *anrongguru* who led the rite said 'let us state our intention that the meal we want to eat may scent the dead, so the dead will be at peace in the *alam barzakh*'. I said gently afterwards, 'Prayers are essentially for the meal that we were about to eat, because the prayers are said to be our expression of gratitude to God. So, may God shower us all (including the family members of the deceased) with His mercy.' A few of them nodded, indicating their agreement, but the majority of them just ignored it.

Pak Syamsuddin went on to explain to me that on every occasion conducted by the Sayyid to which he was invited, he tried by any possible means to translate the essential meaning and proper use of every prayer recited and of each scriptural text used, because for the most part the traditionalists do not know the 'proper' meaning and use of the Qur'anic verses.

Reciting the Qur'an for the benefit of the dead is a commonplace practice in Muslim communities. The modernists strongly object to the assumption that the living can send merit to the dead by performing the Pattumateang. As well, the modernists criticise the traditionalist practice of visiting the tombs of holy ancestors. The modernists also question the capacities of the *anrongguru* beyond the grave.

On the other hand, the traditionalists believe that because the bereaved family are in need of help to perform the prayers, a religious specialist is required and the best is the former *anrongguru* of their parents while alive. It should be noted clearly that this argument never develops into open conflict. One reason is probably because the modernists (mostly members of Muhammadiyah) actually rarely attend Pattumateang ceremonies. As one modernist put it to me, 'if we come we must eat and drink, and that is unlawful, so it is better not to come.'

Overall, the consequence of decades of such arguments over these issues is that many Cikoangese today, especially those residing in Jakarta, are wiser in terms of what is 'Islamic' about their long-standing festivities, particularly with reference to the sources of the Qur'an and Hadith. Despite their frequent reliance in Cikoang on religious practices of Maudu' and Pattumateang, the Sayyid in Jakarta are more flexible and have a different understanding about the grounds for performing the practices than those back in Cikoang. One Sayyid in Jakarta openly acknowledged to me that he personally criticised traditional assumptions, for example, that the Maudu' festival is the most rewarding religious practice in the eyes of Allah and that if one performs Maudu' he or she will be exempt from all other religious duties, including the five daily prayers and the pilgrimage to Mecca. He said:

> Maudu' is a practice symbolising the holiness of the Prophet Muhammad. It is a medium of *dakwah*, so that people will be continuously reminded of the teachings of the Prophet and will copy his example. *Sembahyang* is also another religious practice. Both of these are symbols of devotion.

This Sayyid believed that his relatives in Cikoang were fanatical in following early sayings of the elders, without adopting a critical attitude to scriptural evidence (In. *dalil syar'i*). Yet his firm belief in the pre-existence of the Prophet Muhammad before the creation of the world (Nur Muhammad) and the possibility of the Sufi attainment of union with Allah (a la Tarekat Bahr ul-Nur) remained unchanged.

Another interesting point is that, in principle, Maudu' is said to be valid (In. *sah*) only if it is celebrated in Cikoang. Yet the Cikoangese in Jakarta are able to excuse themselves from coming to Cikoang for the celebration of the Maudu'. If they are under constraints of finance or time, those living in Jakarta have no strict obligation to carry out the rituals. What they can do is to entrust to someone a sum of money for their relatives in Cikoang for the preparations. A Cikoangese calculated the sum of money he sent thus:

> I spent roughly between Rupiah 700,000 and Rupiah 1,000,000 for my Maudu' obligations every year. It was a lot of money, but much cheaper than if I were to make the trip to Cikoang myself.

So the cost of travel back home can also become a convenient excuse for absence from the Maudu' ceremonies.

As for the ritual observation of Pattumateang, the Cikoangese in Jakarta depend on their *anrongguru*, whose residence may be in Kampong Cikoang or in Ujung Pandang. They do not ask their *anrongguru* to come to Jakarta unless they are financially capable of doing so. Those who cannot afford it will ask non-Sayyid religious specialists to proceed with their Pattumateang. Such arrangements suggest that the beliefs and practices of the Cikoangese bring obligations consequent to the power they create, but that they are also dependent on allocations of resources which may not be crippling. Commitments to and from the social body of Cikoang are on the whole very flexible.

CHAPTER SIX
Concluding Remarks

This study has contained two sections. In Part One, Chapters One to Three, we observed that the exclusiveness of the Sayyid community of Cikoang, South Sulawesi is directly derived from the interplay between religious and social constructions. The religious legitimacy of the Sayyid is based on their descent from Sayyid Jalaluddin al-'Aidid in the early 17th century. His origins trace back to the Prophet Muhammad. It is this principle of descent which justifies the religious authority of the Sayyid over the Jawi and other non-Sayyid Makassarese. Strictly speaking, it is broadly held that for anyone to discard the theological decisions of the Sayyid is tantamount to rejecting the teachings of the Prophet himself: to dispute with the Sayyid is improper and to hate them is wrong.

Interestingly, given this obvious prestige, the Sayyid not only eclipse the Jawi in terms of religion but also in realms economic and political. The Sayyid are said to have dominated the election of village heads in the area over decades, particularly in Cikoang itself. The Sayyid are also among the major employers of the local people; the evidence for this can be easily found in Cikoang, Ujung Pandang and Jakarta.

It is the valuing of descent which underlies the Sayyid practice of *kafa'ah* in choosing marriage matches. To keep the bloodlines pure, they protect their daughters from marrying non-Sayyid men, in the knowledge that such marriages would disjoint their ties with the Prophet and lead to a state of impurity. The reverse principle does not apply to sons. Since it is through them that Sayyid status passes, they are freer in their choice of brides.

In Part Two of this study, Chapters Four and Five, the religious debate between conservative Cikoangese and the Muhammadiyah movement was discussed. Arguments originally derived from the question of who is right and wrong in their Islamic practices. Those who side with the unchanged practices of the past are labelled 'traditionalists' and those who stand for reform are called 'modernists'.

Many Indonesianists believe that religion in Indonesia has today become susceptible to ideals of literacy, nationalism and modernity. Those who follow local beliefs and customs may be considered to be people who 'do not yet have a religion' (In. *belum beragama*) or at least do not practise a complete implementation of their chosen faith. Waterson (1989) has observed a strong pressure for traditional beliefs to be redefined within the terms of the world religions, or for drawing a clear line of demarcation between local traditions and the 'proper' practice of the embraced religion.

On the other hand, the government must curb sentiments of extremism – especially Islamic extremism – while precluding any condemnation of 'over-secularising' the Indonesian people. This range of religious phenomena demonstrates the variety of manifestations of the world religions in Indonesia, within which Islam might have been seen to exist merely as a 'layer' superimposed on top of earlier traditions (Waterson 1989: 115). Under this paradigm the superimposition of, or juxtaposition between, Islam and local practice becomes evident in many parts of the Indonesian archipelago.

Many Indonesianists, both Indonesian and non-Indonesian, have explored the dynamic aspects of religions in modern Indonesia. The world religions are often viewed as transformations of each other or of other cultural domains (In. *adat*) (see Geertz 1960, 1984; and Woodward 1989 for Java; Abdullah 1966 for Minangkabau; Pelras 1985 for Makassar; and Kipp and Rodgers 1987). In other words, many Indonesian people would seem to profess syncretic beliefs.

Pelras (1985) regards such syncretic beliefs among the Makassarese to be the result of the penetration of Islam into local tradition, or *adat*, during the earliest period of its expansion. The current dispute regarding 'proper' Islamic practices between traditionalists and modernists in the religious arena of Cikoang is to be seen in this light. The tendency of Muslims in the 'periphery' to perpetuate their Islamic conduct, which they see as partner to their local tradition, is confronted by the modernists who insist upon the implementation of more orthodox practices.

The modernists maintain that the Cikoangese Muslims carry out their Islamic duties while still adhering to their local customs. They see the traditionalist practices as *bid'ah*, or heretical innovation. For instance, the traditionalist

Cikoangese hold that the celebration of the Prophet Muhammad's birth is the main tenet of their Islam on the grounds that the Prophet and Allah are one in mystical terms. They give precedence to the veneration of the Prophet and of their Sufi masters, the *anrongguru*, above any other observance.

This is obvious during the Maudu' festival, which the Cikoangese believe is the time of obtaining *barakka* (Mak.; Ar. *barakah*; In. *berkah*) or Allah's blessing through the spirit of the Prophet. They also regularly visit the graves of their ancestors, bringing flowers and other offerings and burning incense to request *washilah* (Ar.; In. *perantaraan*), intermediary action or intercession in order to obtain blessings from Allah. This custom of visiting graves is mostly directed not towards spiritual communion but towards requests for prosperity and good fortune for themselves.

There are wider perspectives to all of this. Such visitations, or *ziarah*, are undertaken throughout the Muslim world, from Morocco to Indonesia, where the tombs of the saints are believed to be places to gain Allah's blessing (Woodward 1989: 68–69). Makruf (1995) identifies this visiting of a sacred tomb in the Javanese context as a way of linking one's 'intellectual chain' to the holy saints, for example, the Wali who brought Islam to Java. Makruf explains that in Javanese *nyekar* ('to strew flowers') is a synonym for *ziarah*, as is the term *sowan*, but this is more correctly understood as the visiting of a living person of higher social status in consultation of some matter. Makruf differentiates *ziarah* from *nyekar* and *sowan*: *ziarah* is carried out with the hope of gaining *barakah* through the mediation of the Wali, while *nyekar* and *sowan* indicate more material intentions. In Cikoang the practice of *ziarah* and the Pattumateang, or the ritual prayers for the dead, are other main issues of dispute between traditionalists and modernists.

Within the viewpoint of the modernists, Islam has to be purified from all pagan practices, such as any kind of veneration of the ancestors in asking Allah's blessings. These practices go against the authority of Allah as the only supernatural being to whom human beings should ask for reward, they maintain, and Islam discourages the use of *washilah* to importune Allah. The modernists view the practices of the Muslims in Cikoang as being nothing less than *shirk* or *musyrik* (Ar.; polytheism, the fundamental sin of associating other supernaturalities beside Allah). The modernists' point of view is undoubtedly based on the Qur'an itself, Surah *al-Ikhlas* (Sincerity) verse 112, which reads in its entirety:

> Say: He is God, the One. God, the Eternal.
> He begot not nor was He begotten.
> And there is none comparable beside Him.

This short Surah is frequently recited in worship. It is the fundamental statement of the oneness of Allah and it brings the Muslims of Cikoang onto the horns of a dilemma: whether to follow the modernists' version of a 'pure' Shariah implementation of Islam, or to perpetuate their own practices associated with Sufi doctrines and local usages.

The argument is unsurprisingly not limited to the Cikoangese. We can find similar cases throughout the Indonesian archipelago, such as among the Minangkabau of West Sumatra.[1] Many Muslim scholars have weighed into the dispute between modernists and traditionalists. For instance, the famous *ulama* Haji Abdul Malik Karim Amrullah, popularly known as 'Buya' Hamka, adopted his father's solution regarding the local traditions of Minangkabau. Hamka is one of the modernist figures of Indonesia who has tended not to fight all traditional values, as many others did. One of Buya Hamka's (1984: 105–106) remarks is expressed in the following poem of the relationship between Syari'at, Islamic law, and *adat*, or local custom:

> *Adat bersendi Syara'*
> *Syara' bersendi Kitabullah*
> *Syara' mengata, Adat memakai*
> *Syara' bertelanjang, Adat bersesamping*
> *Adat menurun, Syara' menaik*

> Custom is based on the Law
> The Law is based on the Qur'an
> The Law states, Custom applies
> The Law is bare, Custom is well-clothed
> Custom descends, the Law rises above

This poem affirms that *adat* and Syari'at are closely related, as in the union of milk and water, rather than opposed entities. Indonesianists agree that *adat* and Syari'at have coexisted since Islam first put down its roots in the Minangkabau region. The thought here is that Syari'at is on the rise, steadily making clearer what is practised. But the verse bears no explicit markers of time, making it susceptible to the reading of a never-ending process in which Islam will continuously collaborate with what is found in local settings.

Kipp and Rodgers (1987) also conclude that in the interaction between Islam and local belief the two become fused. This is further evident in the work of Clifford Geertz on Java (1984: 127) who explores the concept of 'person' according to two sets of differences, one between *inside* and *outside* and the other one between *refined* and *vulgar*. The inside world or *bathin* (originally an Islamic and a Sufi

---

1 See Abdullah 1966..

term) can be achieved through religious exercises, known in Javanese beliefs as *poso* (In. *puasa*) or fasting and *tapa* or *semedi*, both meaning meditation, which then enable the person to control his or her emotional life.

On the other hand, the outside or *lahir* can be achieved through etiquette, which generates the person's social behaviour. The two realms are then put in a separate structure through which the difference between *refined* (In. *halus*) and *vulgar* (In. *kasar*) in the person's disposition will apply. What Geertz found interesting is that there is a 'bifurcated conception' of the person in Java: 'an inner world of stilled emotion and an outer world of shaped behaviour' (1984: 127–128). In Islam, these are also well known as *alam lahir dan bathin*. Most Javanese claim that the *bathin* of a person is far more important than their *lahir*, as it is the locus of divine capability (In. *ilmu bathin* or *ilmu laduni*). The Cikoangese also stress the greater importance of *bathin*. Many Sayyid explained to me that *bathin* is the source of bad and good things both: the good deeds of a person are a reflection of a clean or pure *bathin*, and vice versa.

Many Indonesianists believe that there has been historical interaction between pre- or non-Islamic mystical teachings and Sufism. Woodward (1989) maintains that this interpenetration was actively encouraged by early Muslim missionaries in Java as a bridge to winning converts. Before Islam became the predominant religion, concepts of *tapa* or *semedi* and the acquisition of *sakti*, divine power, originating from Saivite Hinduism were common spiritual goals among the Javanese. Woodward names such interaction as the 'harmonisation' of non-Islamic and Islamic principles.

Woodward then clarifies this process, stressing not how the interaction of non-Islamic elements and Muslim tradition takes place but rather how such elements are Islamically 'interpreted'. His overall point is that much (but not all) that has been considered to be *kejawen*, or Javanese syncretism (e.g. by Clifford Geertz 1984), is actually encompassed by Sufism. One example is the belief in the Prophet Muhammad as the 'Perfect Man' (Ar. *al-Insan al-Kamil*). In another instance, Muhammad is identified as Semar, the most important character in the Javanese *wayang* shadow puppet repertoire. Semar is said to have reached a state of divinity and thus to be the owner of pure *bathin*. Certain Javanese conceive of Semar as *nabi bathin*, the 'inner prophet' and the symbol of the union between humanity and divinity. Yet, because he has a physical shape, as traditionalists put it, he is not completely God. Thus they are precluding condemnations of *shirk* or *musyrik* (Woodward 1989: 223–225).

Throughout the Muslim world, the Sufis are known as those most responsible for popularising the celebration of the Prophet's birth, Maulid Nabi (e.g. Schimmel 1985). The modernists consider this festival to have combined local idioms with

Sufi doctrines. For example, as Maudu' is celebrated by the traditionalists in Cikoang, the local idiom is obvious in the provision of ingredients such as rice, chicken, coconut and egg in Kanre Maudu', the Maulid feast.

However, in Maudu' the use of *julung-julung*, the petty boats to carry the *kandawari* towers of offerings, might be wrongly seen as Cikoangese local usage, considering the fame of the Makassarese as boat builders and seafarers. Rather, the boat is the symbol of salvation both in Sayyid Ahl al-Bait and Sufi traditions. In Cikoang, the *julung-julung* become the symbol of Sayyid *kafa'ah*-based marriage practice that will guarantee salvation in this world and the hereafter (see Chapter Three). According to the traditionalists, the symbol of the boat also refers to the ark built by the Prophet Nuh, or Noah, to rescue living creatures at the time when flood inundated all parts of the world.

What is similar to Woodward's (1989) position is that the Cikoangese beliefs and practices have demonstrable roots in the Sufi traditions, rather than being evidence of a resilience of pre-Islamic beliefs and practices. When it comes to the Muslim modernists, their primary objection seems to rest more on the fact that certain Sufi beliefs and practices – especially modes of veneration of the Prophet – are not doctrinally orthodox according to their criteria, i.e. are not ratified by the Syari'at, however much their own Syari'at practices may have been inflected by local idiom as well.

So the main point of difference between the modernists and the traditionalists lies in the significance of the ritual objects used in the Maudu' festival. The traditionalists believe that the inclusion of rice, chickens, coconut and eggs in the ritual of the shared meal is the only way, the obligatory way, to express their religious faith. They will feel humiliated if they do not do this, whereas the modernists are more flexible in this matter and are not restricted to particular ingredients.

Moreover, the modernists maintain that the main aspect of the celebration lies in the fact that it can be an occasion for the propagation of the Prophet's teachings. The modernists have free choice in this, since the Maudu' festival is not *fardhu* or *wajib*, obligatory under the law. It is not even *sunnah*, optional, but meritorious if performed. The central concern, then, is with the difference between the two parties in their respective construction of meanings around the Maudu' and how its observance achieves the objectives of the celebration.

The modernists agree that the Prophet Muhammad is a figure worthy of veneration. Practices instructed by him can led to a mystical experience that leads the human heart to the key of nearness to Allah. In the Sufi doctrines, the veneration of the Prophet is the basis of the doctrine of Nur Muhammad, the divine light of Muhammad and his pre-existence with creation (Schimmel 1985).

6. Concluding Remarks

What the modernists object to is the concept that the unity of the Prophet and Allah is paralleled by a Sufi unity of humanity to Allah, because this can lead to *shirk* or *musyrik* (Woodward 1989: 237).

In a final note, the modernists maintain that Muslims should base their religious practice on the scriptures – the Qur'an, Hadith and the Syari'at – whereas the traditionalists study Sufi doctrines as the basis for their religious practices. Syari'at-minded Muslims (or Scripturalists) and the Sufis have been two of the most significant agents in the development of Muslim tradition. Frequently they work together; at other times they are at odds.

Principally, the nature of debate between Syari'at and Sufism is that the Sufis tend to stress the mediation and veneration of saints or holy persons for asking Allah's rewards while minimising the significance of the law. The Sufis also give precedence to the importance of obtaining union between Allah and the individual human soul, no matter what method this might involve. As Gilsenan (1973: 5) puts it 'there are as many paths to God as there are children of Adam'.

Syari'at-minded Muslims, on the contrary, emphasise the implementation of their version of 'pure' Islamic practices in submission to Allah's will, so much so that they may be called *kaum puritan*, or 'puritans'. They believe that it is by performing the prescribed practices in a 'proper' way (according to the Syari'at) that nearness to Allah can be achieved. There is covert agreement here: both Sufism and the Syari'at aim *in principle* to come close to Allah; their differences lie in the course of implementation.

In the case of Sufism in Cikoang, the Cikoangese follow one of the many different kinds of orders as their *tarekat*, their 'pathway'. There is no need to seek a definition between 'proper' and 'improper' Sufi orders in terms of practice, because what is substantive behind the term *tarekat* is 'a variety of religious groupings bearing a variety of social meanings and functions in a variety of social, economic and political settings' (Gilsenan 1973: 5). Judging from most of the Sufi doctrines I have enquired into there does indeed exist a great variety, yet in Indonesia each generates from the same concept of the Divine Light of Muhammad. Thus, notions of process or *tarekat* may vary, but all are generally defended by reference to conventional sources based on recognisable, related utterances.

The Cikoangese living in Jakarta, despite their adherence to the practices of *kafa'ah*, Maudu' and Pattumateang, are able to adopt a more critical attitude towards their religious orientation than their relatives in Cikoang. They are more tolerant of criticism from the modernists. They have allowed the establishment of a Muhammadiyah sub-branch in their settlement, which has not been the case in Cikoang. Due to the shortage of Sayyid there, they rarely obtain teachings of Sufism from the Sayyid, their religious specialists at home (see Table 5). They obtain most of their knowledge from followers of other Sufi orders and general books on the subject, or they make a focused study of books telling of classical Sufi scholars such as Jalaluddin Rumi, Imam al-Ghazali, Ibn al-'Arabi and al-Hallaj.

There are at least two further findings that I drew from observing the Cikoangese in Jakarta: first, their knowledge of Sufism is no longer derived from an uncritical acceptance of theological decisions of their elders. One Sayyid Tuan, a holder of a university bachelor's degree and employed in Jakarta, said to me:

> I am lucky that I no longer live in Cikoang. I would not be progressing as I feel I am now if I had not left Cikoang. Due to a lack of learning on Sufism of their own, the people there exaggerate Maudu' as the only religious practice most highly rewarded by Allah. Therefore, they emphasise the ritual aspect of the celebration rather than its mystical aspect. Now (I know that) doing contemplation can bring us close to Allah.

He then acknowledged that he prayed regularly five times a day, that he had made the pilgrimage to Mecca and he undertook other formal duties as did many Indonesian Muslims, while at the same time studying Sufism. For him, the practices set out by Syari'at and Sufism are all equally symbols of piety. My second finding is that, partly due to a declining sense of moral obligation and because of financial constraints, many Cikoangese in Jakarta feel less inclined to make the journey back to Cikoang to participate in the Maudu' festival.

Since opportunities to study the Muslim scriptures of the Qur'an and Hadith and Sufism are at present available everywhere, more and more Indonesian Muslims, including the Cikoangese in Jakarta, no longer rely for resolution of their religious questions solely on the capability of their traditional teachers. Particularly in Jakarta, many Islam-oriented foundations provide courses on Sufism. There is more opportunity for the Cikoangese to study Sufism for themselves. Many young Cikoang people in Jakarta feel that there is no need to enter into the long-lasting relationship of student and teacher. They still, however, maintain the Sufi ethos while focusing on the content of the doctrines.

To sum up concisely, the debate between modernists and traditionalists is an unending religious conversation. New political circumstances and conditions of modernity, as found in Jakarta, arise to affect the debate. Yet this does not mean that the Sayyid will eventually lose their identity either because of urbanisation or strong opposition by the modernists. Rather, *kafa'ah*, the Maudu' festival and the Pattumateang remain strong among the Cikoangese in Jakarta. Patji (1991: 158) observed that the Sayyid always manage to interact with the changing situations of Indonesian life. Their social integration is a 'continuing phenomenon'.

6. Concluding Remarks

In addition and contra to the above, there has been a growing concern among the Cikoangese in Jakarta to adjust their traditional beliefs and practices by means of publishing the doctrines of Tarekat Bahr ul-Nur in printed form and circulating them among the heads of households. The production of these written teachings is intended to refresh and represent Sayyid Sufi orientation in the light of scholarly and modern thought and in order to emphasise the balance between the ritual and contemplative aspects of their Sufi practices.

In 1984 Tuan Hasan and other Cikoangese in Jakarta presented a replica of the Maudu' festival in Taman Mini Indonesia Indah (TMII), the Indonesian cultural theme park in Jakarta in 1984. He said that the 1984 occasion was held to introduce the festival to the people of Jakarta in the hope that it would eventually be recognised as one of the Indonesian Islamic traditions, and therefore should be preserved.

In the present day, the Indonesian government, notably the local authority in Ujung Pandang, has officially recognised the Maudu' festival as an integral part of South Sulawesi tradition. The celebration of Maudu' in Cikoang is said to have become one of the most popular tourist attractions and has supported the regional income of the Ujung Pandang authority in recent years. These opportunities have inspired the Cikoangese in South Sulawesi and in Jakarta to maintain the central practices of their faith and identity, even as they change in tune with contemporary Indonesian society.

APPENDICES

APPENDIX I

Types of *Lontara'*: The Bugis-Makassar Manuscripts

Lontara' are the traditional texts handwritten in the Bugis-Makassar language and script. According to most scholars (e.g. Matthes 1874; Cense 1951; Noorduyn 1961, 1965; Abidin 1971; Pelras 1985; Caldwell 1988), the word *lontara'* is derived from Java or Bali and outside South Sulawesi. Matthes (1874) in particular believed that *lontara'* is derived from the Javanese and Malay word *lontar*, itself being a 'transposition' of *rontal* – literally meaning 'whose leaves could be written upon with a stylus'.[1] The script of *lontara'* manuscripts used in South Sulawesi is called *urupu sulapa' eppa'*, or square letters.

The *lontara'* consist of several types according to their subject matter (Zainal Abidin 1971: 159–160). The first are *attoriolong*, telling of people of former times and containing historical facts. The second are the *lontara' bilang* (also called *Kotika*). These are almanacs for determining auspicious and inauspicious dates and times of undertakings as well as diaries of the rulers of South Sulawesi kingdoms.[2] The third are the *lontara' ada'* in Makassar, or *ade'* in Bugis, containing notes on *adat*, or customary law, namely *rapang* in Makassar areas and *latowa* in Bugis. The fourth type are the *lontara' ulu ada* (Bugis) or *ulukanaya* (Makassar) consisting of texts of treaties with surrounding empires or

---

1   According to Matthes (1874), *lontar* was a 'combination of the Javanese words *ron* (leaf) and *tal*, a particular kind of tree, *Borassus flabelliformis*. This tree is called *ta'* in Bugis, *tala'* in Makassarese and *tala* in Sanskrit. According to Matthes again, *lontara'* meant first the leaf of the *lontar* tree and eventually any written work' (cf. Abidin 1971).
2   According to Noorduyn (1965: 142) the only diary edited for academic use is that of the kings of Gowa and Tallo', covering the period of the 17th century and the first half of the 18th century.

with overseas countries. The fifth are called the *lontara' allopi-lopi*, collections of *adat* law recording shipping, weapons and other property. Finally, there are the *lontara' pangoriseng*, literally meaning the genealogies of the various rulers.[3]

Despite the many different kinds of *lontara'*, the largest contain notes regarding historical accounts. These notes are occasionally grouped together in small collections called *tolo'*. The *tolo'*, in older times, were usually chanted accompanied by a kind of violin called *keso-keso* in honour of the king's arrival. The *tolo'* tell of the enormity of famous warriors' struggles with enemy military; for example the *tolo'na Bone*, which recounts the opposition of the Bone kingdom to the Dutch in 1905 (Abidin 1971).

There is also another massive written chronicle called *I La Galigo*, which according to the Luwu' nobility (the cradle of South Sulawesi aristocracy) is also said to be a *lontara'* chronicle. Yet, as Abidin (1971: 161) has argued, the 'literary' *I La Galigo* is not similar to other *lontara'*. The content of the *I La Galigo* is derived from oral traditions, mostly containing mythical elements. The *I La Galigo* provides support for the belief that the early rulers and founders of the people of South Sulawesi descended from the sky, traditionally known as *Tomanurung*. This myth is then generally incorporated into every *lontara'* chronicle (Noorduyn 1965: 138).

Nevertheless, the myths were given less priority by the writers of *lontara'* than the material contained in *I La Galigo*. The authors and interpreters of *lontara'*, called *Palontara'* or official writers tended to provide historical facts, including the myth of Tomanurung, in a common-sense way (Noorduyn 1965). Zainal Abidin (1971) has suggested that we should not leave out the *I La Galigo* entirely, since it serves as the 'main source' of the history of Bugis before the 14th century.[4] In other words, *I La Galigo* provides the primary background to the writing of the *lontara'* which came into being in the following centuries.[5]

---

3   Abidin (1971: 160) also points out that the term *lontara'* applies as well to traditional manuals, such as those on agriculture, *lontara' pallaoruma*, and on medical lore, *lontara' pabbura*.
4   'Certainly this work must rank among the longest pieces of literature in the world – European scholars alone assembled about 6,000 folio pages of it (this does not include the large number of folio pages still dispersed within the Bugis community)'. Friedericy (1933) has said: 'Ethnologically, it is, without any doubt, the most valuable piece contained in the two chrestomathies of Matthes' (Kern 1954; Matthes 1864–1872: 416–537, notes 250–253; cf. Abidin 1971).
5   The *lontara'* chronicles only came into existence in the 17th century. Noorduyn has pointed out that 'the Indian origin of the script shows that the art of writing was known before the introduction of Islam in the early seventeenth century; for, had the Bugis or Makassar no system of writing at the time, they would surely have adopted the Jawi-Malay script' (1962: 31; cf. Caldwell 1988: 11). What is more, *lontara'* were widely used well into the 20th century by various other languages of Sulawesi: Mandar, Duri, Enrekang and Toraja, and also in Bima. See further Abidin 1971.

Problems of utilising the *lontara'* as historical sources

The *lontara'* basically lack precisely documented sources of South Sulawesi history before the 17th century (see Abidin 1971). The content of the *lontara'* is therefore derived from oral traditions and the *I La Galigo* in the documenting of the previous events. These oral traditions, in fact, contain some mythical elements – *I La Galigo* contains myths expressed in poetical forms, which are passed on through one generation to another in time and space. Myth tends to dominate when a story is written down generations after the events and has survived as oral memory.

In that sense, the *lontara'* cannot conceal or cause a fading away of myths; for example, the legendary tale of the Tomanurung, the first ruler of the Makassar kingdom, is found in the chronicles (Abidin 1971: 166). Yet, the *lontara'* scribes tended to write 'the Tomanurung, whose origin is never known', instead of writing 'the one(s) who descended from the sky' as the authors of *I La Galigo* did.

Another historical myth found in the *lontara'*, and the main theme of this study, is the documentation of the Islamisation of South Sulawesi. According to the Lontara' Bilang, the diary of the kings of Gowa and Tallo', the first person who embraced Islam was the ruler of Tallo' and the chancellor of Gowa. However, some oral traditions, generally found in Luwu, state that it was a person called Tenriajeng, also known as I Assalang (the First) and Tenripau (Not-to-be-mentioned) who became the first local Muslim in South Sulawesi. Thus caution is recommended when utilising the *lontara'* in historical inquiry of South Sulawesi, because the sources adopted by the authors derived from oral traditions which may vary from one locality to another and contain myths.

From the above problems, we probably can see why the historian Soedjatmoko (1965) believed that 'for quite some time the Indonesian historian will be confronted with demands for corroborative evidence for existing myths or for new myths, as well as for a historiography to justify them. The strong disposition to mythologise and to see a moral significance between events that are not necessarily related at all,' according to this writer, are due to 'a historical attitude of Indonesian traditional culture and its continuing impact in an environment of self-activated revolutionary mass democracy'. The solution to the problem, as Soedjatmoko proposed, lies in 'faithful observance of the critical method in handling source materials, "meticulous attention" to detail' and 'the disciplining of historical imagination' (Soedjatmoko 1965: 405, 412).

Another solution is also applicable; namely, the use of 'backdating' first introduced by Crawford (1820; cf. Caldwell 1988). By using the royal genealogies and chronicles, Crawford, and later Ian Caldwell took a 'known and securely dated person late in genealogy and by "backdating", using a fixed number of years for each generation, a chronological framework could then be obtained for earlier individuals and events. The scattered information accompanying various individuals in these and other sources can then be placed within this framework' (Caldwell 1988: 164–165).[6]

A good example of the backdating method is provided by the well-documented conversion to Islam of the rulers of Gowa and Tallo' (1605 CE) and other major kingdoms in the first two decades of the 17th century. An article written by Noorduyn (1956) sets precisely the exact year at 1605 CE, which is officially used by most historians nowadays as the starting point of the conversion of South Sulawesi at large.

---

6   'Genealogies provide a useful means for double checking the contents of the chronicles. If a discrepancy exists, obviously the historian must examine all the evidence even more closely. The importance of checking the genealogies can be seen in an example in Noorduyn's dissertation.' (Abidin 1971: 168–169).

APPENDIX II
The Tale of the Three Datok

The arrival of the Three Datok, if we refer to the Kutei Chronicle, was around 1575. One of them, Datok ri Bandang, was well known in the area as Tuan di Bandang and was believed to have come to South Sulawesi with a colleague named Tuan di Parangan in order to introduce Islam to the local people, but they were unsuccessful. However in about 1600, according to the text of *'Lontara' Sukku'na Wajo'*, the Malay community asked the Three Datok to come again to Makassar. Again they failed to convert any of the high aristocrats. Following that failure, they decided to leave for Luwu' to convert the aristocrats there (Pelras 1985: 112).

Pelras hypothesises that the change of route of the Three Datok's mission was not solely intended to Islamise the Luwu' nobility, but more substantially because Luwu' was known as the 'cradle of South Sulawesi nobility' and the 'central place of the myth of origin.' If Luwu' were the first Islamised, then it would open the whole of South Sulawesi to Islam; so Luwu' was regarded as the 'key strategic point' (Pelras 1985: 119–120). At that time, as in modern Makassar and particularly in the rural areas today, the division of social strata in the community of Gowa was a predominant factor in the culture, economy and religion.

This system can be divided into three groups as follows: Anak karaeng ri Gowa (the children of Gowa ruler); Tumaradeka (the free people); and Ata (the slaves) (Patunru 1983: 139). The latter two classes were subordinate to the former. Thus, whatever aristocrats habitually did, their society would assume such conduct to be a good model. Datok ri Bandang approached the Makassar nobility first and introduced the Islamic faith to them. In due course they succeeded in converting the ruler of the kingdom of Tallo' and the Prime Minister of Gowa, Karaeng Matoaya, to Islam.

APPENDIX III

The Kinship Terms of the Cikoangese

The domains of Sayyid kin relationships are designated by the following terms: *sikalabini* or nuclear family, the husband and wife with their children, *bija pammanakang*, defined as kindred, and *bija panrenrengang*, all individuals counted in a kin group through marriage or affines. Individuals who are not part of this kin relationship are called *tu maraeng,* non-relatives, or what Chabot (1996) called *tu pantara,* outsiders.

These kinship terms are much like those used in Makassar and those below are largely adopted and reworked from Chabot (1996: 89). It is worth noting that *bura'ne* refers to male and *baine* refers to female; for instance, *ana'* (child) *bura'ne* and *ana' baine*. Individuals in category no. 6 below are often called *bungko* (In. *bungsu*), meaning 'youngest'. Those in categories 1 to 6 are called *sikalabini*; those in categories 7 to 29 are *bija pammanakang* and those in categories 30 to 33 are *bija panrenrengang*.

Table 6: Kinship terms

1. Father: *mangge, bapa', ajji* and *tetta*.
2. Mother: *anrong, amma'*.
3. Brother: *sari'battang bura'ne*.
4. Sister: *sari'battang baine*.
5. The eldest brothers and sisters of 3 and 4: *sari'battang kaminang toa*.
6. The youngest brothers/sisters of 3 and 4: *sari'battang kaminang lolo*.
7. Brothers and sisters of 1 and 2: *purina*
8. Children of 7: *samposikali*
9. Fathers and mothers of 1 and 2: *toa*
10. Brothers and sisters of 9: *toa*
11. Children of 10: *purina*
12. Children of 11: *sampopinruang*
13. Fathers and mothers of 9: *boe*
14. Brothers and sisters of 13: *boe*
15. Children of 14: *toa*
16. Children of 15: *purina*
17. Children of 16: *sampopintallung*
18. Son: *ana' bura'ne*
19. Daughter: *ana' baine*
20. Children of 18 and 19: *cucu*
21. Children of 3 and 4: *kamanakang*
22. Children of 21: *cucu*
23. Children of 8: *kamanakang*
24. Children of 23: *cucu*
25. Children of 12: *kamanakang*
26. Children of 25: *cucu*
27. Children of 17: *kamanakang*
28. Children of 27: *cucu*
29. Children of 20, 22, 24, 26, 28: *cucu kulantu'*
30. Spouses of 3, 4, 5 and 6: *ipara*
31. Parents of spouses: *matoang*
32. Spouses of 18 and 19: *mintu*
33. Individuals of 30: *lago*

Source: After Chabot 1996: 89.

APPENDIX IV

Subdivisions of the Anakkaraeng

The Makassar aristocracy are often categorised as Anakkaraeng, literally, children of Sombaya ri Gowa, Karaeng, ruler or chief of the kingdom of Gowa. Within this top social stratum, there are four clusters based on the 'proportion of white (noble) blood as against the red blood of commoners'. They are as follows:

a. *Anak tiknok*: the pure aristocrats, their blood undiluted by commoners' blood. They consists of two status levels: *Anak tiknok pattola*, possessing the highest title among the *Anakkaraeng*; and the *Anak Manrapik*, who could obtain the highest title when no appropriate *Anak tiknok* was available.

b. *Anak Sipuew*: those having mixed blood of Tumanurung and commoners. They were divided into *Anak Sipuwe Manrapik*, who like the *Anak tiknok manrapik* could receive a highest title when the *Anak tiknok* lacked candidates; and the *Anak sipuwe*, persons who had mother of *Ata nibuang* (slave) (see below) and father of the *Anak tiknok pattola*.

c. *Anak cerak*: persons who had a mother of any status level of the Ata and a father of at least *Anak sipuwe manrapik*.

d. *Anakkaraeng sala*. The father inherited the blood of *Anak sipuwe* or *Anak cerak*, whereas the mother had either commoner's or slave's blood. At present they form the majority of the Anakkaraeng.

In sum, the Anakkaraeng and its various ranks consist of those who can trace their origins to the supposed founders of the Gowa kingdom, the 'white-blooded' Tumanurung. According to Bulbeck (1992: 41) 'the aristocrats were ranked by the degree to which their white blood, as traced through both parents, remained undiluted by the red blood of commoners; access to titles depended on nobility of birth. That is, status was ascribed.' In the 15th and 16th centuries only pure descendants reserved the right to rule a kingdom (Friedericy 1933; Mukhlis 1975; Acciaioli 1989; cf. Bulbeck 1992: 41). Nonetheless, among the Makassarese a patrilateral bias existed from the essentially bilateral manner of ascribing status (Röttger-Rössler 1989: 42–43; Mukhlis 1975: 37–38; cf. Bulbeck 1992: 281).

APPENDIX V

The Ata, or Slaves, of South Sulawesi

The definition of Ata varies in ethnographic accounts of Makassar. The term means un-free people or slaves. Bulbeck (1992), in particular, divided them into several categories as follows:

a. *Ata sossorang*, the bequeathed slaves whose parents (both father and mother) were formerly slaves.

b. *Ata niballi* (literally, those selling themselves). Individuals became slaves by selling themselves or their children voluntarily to avoid famine or simply putting themselves under the patronage of a chief. In practice, however, people did not agree with the idea of selling slaves. The common way for a master to get rid of a slave he no longer wanted was to command the slave to become a 'debt-bondsman'. The former master borrowed a sum of money of a person and the slave had to work for the person, who then became his new master, until the money had been paid off. Usually, the slave remained with his new master because his former master kept adding to the debt.

c. *Ata nibuang*, individuals becoming a slaves as prisoners of war or because of serious violations of customary law; for example, incest, adultery, thieving, *annyala* (elopement, or thwarting an arranged marriage), and what Bulbeck mentioned as *siri'*, the parameter of the enhancement and degradation of self-respect, self-worth or self-esteem of a person (see below) (Mukhlis 1975: 27–32; Daeng Patunru 1983: 139; Maeda 1984; Röttger-Rössler 1989: 28; cf. Bulbeck 1992: 40–42).

Despite the many different status levels of the Ata, the first three generations are considered as bequeathed slaves, thereafter the Ata were categorised as mere *Ata sossorang* (hereditary slaves).

The Ata, known in present times as *Ata sossorong*, have mixed with the Tumaradeka and are now socially welcomed. Yet, their social role seems to be the lowest among the Tumaradeka. They depend for their subsistence mainly on fishing, agriculture and other manual work. The majority of them (as the offspring of former slaves) are still working in places today owned by their Karaeng (their parents' former masters). The reason why they remain there is unclear: whether it is an expression of gratitude to their Karaeng or because they have no other choice.

According to the historical records, unlike in Java and Madura, the implementation of the official abolition of slavery in South Sulawesi (particularly Makassar) was relatively late. The *Regeerings Reglement*, the Dutch colonial constitution, carried out a decree on 1 January 1860 calling for the abolition of slavery in the entire Netherlands Indies (Reid 1983: 5). However, many Karaeng in South Sulawesi refused to free their Ata. The reason was that, perhaps like helots, the majority of the Ata were working in the farming fields of the Karaeng. They numbered roughly hundreds per estate.

The Karaeng were not persuaded by the call for the abolition of slavery, fearing that their fields would be left in an unfinished state. Therefore, the Governor-General reluctantly stated that the abolition of slavery was only applied to the trade in slaves and implicitly let the existing slaves remain under the possession of their Karaeng. So, the practice of slavery continued to exist in South Sulawesi, even outside the region, until the 1900s (Reid 1983).

Glossary

abbajik	'making good'; the processes of reconciliation for a marriage socially inappropriately contracted in South Sulawesi
adat (Ar., In.)	customary law of place, in contradistinction to Islamic law
Ahl al-Bait (Ar.)	'People of the House'; members of the Prophet Muhammad and his family: his daughter Fatimah and son-in-law Ali and their two sons Hasan and Husein, the latter especially venerated within Shi'ism
alam barzakh (Ar.)	the zone between death and the final judgment of the soul
Al-Irshad	Jami'at al-Islam wal-Irshad al-Arabiya; Association of Islam and Arab Guidance, reformist association founded in Jakarta in 1913
ana'guru (Mak.)	students of the *anrongguru*
Anakkaraeng (Mak.)	descendants of the Ruler of Gowa, hence, the aristocracy of South Sulawesi
a'rate (Mak.)	reciting the Barazanji (q.v.). A chorus of readers recites by turns and then collectively. Performances may last for hours
anrongguru (Mak.)	traditional religious teachers and specialists, usually drawn from the Sayyid and for the Sayyid
Ata (Bug., Mak.)	slave, member of the lowest class of South Sulawesi
Bahr ul-Nur (Ar.)	'The Sea of Light', the mystical path and discipline followed in Cikoang

barakah (Ar.), *barakka* (Mak.), *berkah* (In.)	divine blessings or mercy
Barazanji (Ar.)	genre of songs in praise of the Prophet Muhammad and his life
bembengan (Mak.)	carried litters of offerings used during the Maudu' ceremonies
bid'ah (Ar.)	heretical innovation not ratified by the Qur'an and Hadith (a modernist definition); practices condemned by modernist Muslims
bulang panyongko (Mak.)	the month of preparations before Maulid/Maudu'
caritana turioloa (Mak.)	'stories of the elders'; traditional histories of Cikoang
dakwah (Ar.)	mission, preaching, predication, Islamic outreach
Dato' Tallua (Mak.) Dato' Tellue (Bug.)	the 'Three Teachers' from Minangkabau, Sumatra who introduced Islam into South Sulawesi, c. 1575
fiqh (Ar.) *fiqih* In.)	jurisprudence, legal prescriptions
ganrang (Mak.)	drum, the playing of which is an integral part of aristocratic Makassar wedding celebrations
Hadith (Ar.)	Traditions, the accounts of the words and deeds of Muhammad transmitted through a chain of narrators; with the Qur'an form the sources of Islamic law
Hadhramaut (Ar.)	the southern coastal region of Yemen; the region of origin of the Sayyid of Cikoang
Hadhramis	many of whom migrated to Indonesia; Hadhramis were known as a sophisticated people – traders, intellectuals and holy men – and were prominent in the spread of the Shafi'i school of law in Indonesia
hajj (Ar.) *naik haji* (In.)	the great pilgrimage to Mecca, incumbent on all able Muslims in their lifetime
ijtihad (Ar.)	independent judgment based on recognised sources of Islam on a legal or theological question, approved by modernists in contrast to traditionalist *taqlid* (q.v.)
IPKA	Ikatan Pemuda Keluarga al-'Aidid; Association of Al-'Aidid Family Youth

IPPA	Ikatan Pemuda-Pemudi Al-'Aidid; Al-'Aidid Youth Organisation
Jawi (Ar., In.)	'Javanese', term used originating in Mecca to indicate pilgrims from Indonesia; specifically refers to the populace of non-Arab people of Cikoang and was probably imposed by the Sayyid themselves
Jawi Karaeng (Mak.)	those of aristocratic descent but without Sayyid blood
jikkiri (Mak.) *zikir* (Ar.)	the remembrance of God; Sufi practice; specifically the practices around the Maudu' festival in Cikoang
julung-julung (Mak.)	small boats in which the prepared food is placed during Maudu'
kafa'ah (Ar.)	'equality in marriage partners', the prohibition upon Sayyid women against marrying men of lesser religious rank, thus guaranteeing the Sayyid descent of their children
kanre Maudu' (Mak.)	bamboo baskets of the food prescribed for the Maudu' festival
Karaeng (Mak.)	the original nobility of Makassar
Kerukunan Keluarga Al-'Aidid (In.)	organisation of Al-'Aidid Family Harmony
lontara' (Bug., Mak.)	manuscript literature containing mythology, genealogy, history and traditional sciences
madhhab (Ar.)	school of law; there are four schools in Sunni Islam (see Syafi'i); the schools of Shi'ism differ from these
ma'rifatullah (Ar.)	Islamic gnosis, the direct experience of God
Maudu' (Ar.)	term referring to the celebration of the birth of the Prophet Muhammad, similarly Maulid
Maulid Nabi (Ar.)	the celebration of the birth of the Prophet Muhammad, believed to have been on the 12th day of the month of Rabi'ul Awwal
modernist	reformist Islam, see also Muhammadiyah
muballigh (Ar.)	missionary among Muslims to improve Islamic observance

Muhammadiyah	largest modernist Islamic organisation in Indonesia
Nahdlatul Ulama (NU)	'Revival of the Scholars', Indonesia's largest Islamic organisation, founded to promote traditionalist Islam
Nur Muhammad (Ar.)	'divine light of Muhammad', the essence of one school of Sufism; the doctrine of coevality of creation, Muhammad and the Qur'an
Pangngadakkang (Mak.) Pangngadereng (Bug.)	historical councils of the Ade' (*adat*, q.v.) specialists and the Parewa Sara', Muslim religious authorities in South Sulawesi
Pattumateang (Mak.)	rites for the dead and earlier departed souls, performed in a specific way in Cikoang. The purification of the deceased is conducted for 40 days from the third night after burial
qalbu (Ar.)	heart, soul, mind; the faculty that apprehends the divine
Qur'an (Ar.) / Koran	God's word revealed to Muhammad, the supreme source and authority in Islam
sambulayang (Mak.) / *timpalaja* (Bug.)	decorative roof gables on traditional houses; the number and height indicating the social rank of the household
saukang (Mak.)	natural object traditionally considered to contain magical properties or which could ensure the well-being of the community; most often the object is a stone
Sayyid (Ar.)	title of male descendants of the Prophet, a rank jealously guarded (see *kafa'ah*); in the strict sense, those who claim their line of descent through the Prophet's second grandson, Husein
Sayyid Daeng (Mak.)	children of a Sayyid father and a free woman
Sayyid Karaeng (Mak.)	children of a Sayyid father and Karaeng mother; considered the most perfect social stratum in Cikoang, reconciling religious and secular legitimacy inherited from the parents
Sayyid Tuan (Mak.)	'pure' Sayyid; children of both Sayyid and Syarifah descent
salat (Ar.)	the five daily prescribed prayers in Islam

shalawat (Ar.)	recitations in honor of the Prophet and his early Companions
Shariah (Ar.) Syari'at (Mak.)	Islamic law
Shi'ism	the second-largest branch of Islam, the state religion of Iran and one still followed in parts of Yemen
siri' (Bug., Mak.)	an inner state, first indicating social shame and second indicating the values of self-respect or self-worth
Sunni (Ar.)	also Ahl us-Sunnah wal-Jamaah, 'those who follow the tradition of the Prophet and the consensus o f the community'; orthodoxy, the major branch of Islam worldwide
Syafi'i (Ar.)	one of the four Sunni law schools and the one most followed in Indonesia
syahadat (Ar.)	'declaration of the faith', the proclamation of which before witnesses marks conversion to Islam
Syarif (Ar.)	male descendant of the line of the Prophet's elder grandson Hasan, not recognised specifically in this sense in Indonesia where it is equal to Sayyid
Syarifah (Ar.)	title of female descendants of the Prophet, whose marriage matches are carefully guarded to protect the descent of the children (see *kafa'ah*); similarly, Sayyidah
syirk (Ar.)	the sin of ascribing equals to God, thus denying *tauhid* (q.v.)
Sufi (Ar.)	both practitioner of mysticism and as an adjective, mystical
sunrang (Mak.)	bride-price, which amount is heavily dependent upon the social stratum of the woman's kin group; highest among the Anakkaraeng and lowest among the Ata
tafsir (Ar.)	the science of Qur'anic exegesis, interpretation
taqlid (Ar.)	conventional acceptance of legal and theological decisions of scholars and teachers; deemed uncritical by the modernists
talqing (Mak.) *talqin* (Ar.)	'catechism of the dead'; instructions to the dying soul

tadarusan (Ar., Mak.)	recitations of sections of the Qur'an
tarekat (Ar., In.)	the path of mysticism; the method, system or school of guidance for traversing the path
tasawuf (Ar., In.)	mysticism
tauhid (Ar.)	the Islamic concept of the absolute oneness of God
Traditionalist	Islam as implemented in place, incorporating long-received practices
Tubajik (Mak.)	'distinguished people' with peripheral aristocratic lineage
Tumaradeka (Bug., Mak.)	the populace, neither slaves nor of any aristocratic descent
tumassiri' (Mak.)	those whose *siri'* (q.v.) has been offended
tusamarak (Mak.)	commoners within society
ulama (Ar., In.)	Islamic scholars
washilah (Ar.)	the intercession of the saints; see *barakah* and *ziarah*
wudhu' (Ar.)	necessary ablutions before the performance of the *salat*
Zaydi (Ar.)	branch of Shi'ism with some sway in Yemen; because of its compatibility with Sunni Islam, called the 'Fifth Madhhab' to the four Orthodox schools
ziarah (Ar.)	the visitation of graves and tombs of the Muslim saints, a way of gaining God's blessing; see *barakah*

Bibliography

Abaza, Mona 1988, Hadhramaut and the Southeast Asian World: The Kinship System, Social Stratification and Migration. Unpublished review paper. Federal Republic of Germany: University of Bielefeld.

Abdullah, Taufik 1966, Adat and Islam: An Examination of Conflict in Minangkabau. *Indonesia* 2.

Abidin, A.Z. 1971, Notes on the Lontara' as Historical Sources, *Indonesia* 12. Ithaca, New York: Cornell Modern Indonesia Project.

_____ 1974, The I La Galigo Epic Cycle of South Celebes and Its Diffusion,. Translated by C.C. Macknight, *Indonesia* 17.

Abu-Lughod, Lila 1986, *Veiled Sentiments: Honor and Poetry in a Bedouin Society*. Berkeley: University of California Press.

Acciaioli, Gregory L. 1989, Searching for Good Fortune: the Making of a Bugis Shore Community at Lake Lindu, Central Sulawesi. Unpublished PhD thesis. Canberra, ACT: The Australian National University.

Achmad 1995, Adat Istiadat Dan Pranata Sosial Masyarakat Sayyid di Cikoang, Takalar, South Sulawesi. Ujung Pandang: Sarjana Thesis, Fakultas Adab IAIN Alauddin Ujung Pandang.

Adams, Charles C. 1933, *Islam and Modernism in Egypt*. London: Oxford University Press.

Ahmad, Hisyam 1976, *Latar Belakang Sosial Budaya Masyarakat Keturunan Arab dan Sejarah Pertumbuhan dan Perjuangan Partai Arab Indonesia*. Bandung: Lembaga Kebudayaan, Universitas Padjadjaran.

Ahmad, Muhammad 1979/1980, Kelompok Masyarakat Sayyid di Cikoang. *Agama, Budaya dan Masyarakat, Ikhtisar Laporan Hasil-hasil Penelitian.* Jakarta: Badan Penelitian dan Pengembangan Agama, Departemen Agama, RI.

Algadri, Hamid 1984, *Islam Dan Keturunan Arab: Dalam Pemberontakan Melawan Belanda.* Indonesia: Pustaka LP3ES.

Algadri, Hamid 1994, *Dutch Policy Against Islam and Indonesians of Arab Descent in Indonesia*, Pustaka LP3ES Indonesia.

Ali, Mukti 1970, *The Spread of Islam in Indonesia.* Yogyakarta, Indonesia: Yayasan NIDA.

Andaya, Leonard Y. 1979, A Village Perception of Arung Palakka and the Makassar War of 1666–1669, in A. Reid and D. Marr (eds) *Perception of the Past in South East Asia.* Singapore: Asian Studies of Australia.

―――― 1984, Kingship-Adat Rivalry and the Role of Islam in South Sulawesi. *Journal of Southeast Asian Studies*, Volume XV, Number 1, March 1984.

Arnold, T.W. 1913, *The Preaching of Islam.* 2nd ed. London: Constable & Company Ltd.

Atjeh, Aboebakar 1985, *Sekitar Masuknya Islam ke Indonesia.* Cetakan ke 4, Solo: Ramadhani.

Ayoub, Mahmoud 1984, *The Qur'an and its interpreters.* Albany: State University of New York Press.

Badan Statistik Pemerintah Daerah Tk. II, Gowa 1993, *Gowa Dalam Angka.* Sungguminasa-Gowa-Ujung Pandang: BPS.

Baldry, J. 1984, One Hundred Years of Yemeni History 1849–1948. *L'Arabie du Sud II*, J. Chelhod (ed), Paris: Maisonneuve et Larose.

Bott, Elizabeth 1971, *Family and social network: roles, norms and external relationship in ordinary urban families.* Preface by Max Gluckman. 2nd ed. London: Tavistock.

Bowen, John Richard 1993, *Muslims Through Discourse.* New Jersey: Princeton University Press.

Brockelmann, Carl 1898–1902, 1937–1942, *Geschichte der Arabischen Litteratur* (GAL), 2 vols with supplement. The Netherlands: Leiden.

Bujra, Abdalla S. 1971, *The Politics of Stratification, a Study of Political Change in a South Arabian Town.* Oxford: Clarendon Press.

Bulbeck, Francis David 1992, A tale of two kingdoms: The historical archaelogy of Gowa and Tallok, South Sulawesi Indonesia. Unpublished PhD thesis. Canberra, ACT: The Australian National University.

———— 1996, The Politics of Marriage and the Marriage of Polities in Gowa, South Sulawesi, during the 16th and 17th centuries, in James J. Fox and Clifford Sather (eds), *Origins, Ancestry and Alliance: Exploration in Austronesian Ethnography*. Canberra, ACT: Department of Anthropology, Research School of Pacific and Asian Studies, The Australian National University.

Caldwell, Ian 1988, South Sulawesi AD 1300–1600: Ten Bugis Texts. Unpublished PhD thesis. Canberra, ACT: The Australian National University.

Cense, A.A. 1951, Enige aantekeningen over Makassaars-Boeginese geschiedschrijven. *BKI* 107: 42-60.

Chabot, Hendrick Theodorus 1996, *Kinship, Status and Gender in South Celebes*. Introduction by Martin Rossler and Birgitt Rottger-Rossler-Leiden: KITLV (Koninklijk Instituut Voor Taal, Land-en Volkenkunde), Translation Series 25.

Chelhod, J. 1984, Problemes d'Anthropologie Culturelle Sud-Arabe. *L'Arabie du Sud*; *Histoire et Civilisation,* Tome I, J. Chelhod (ed), Paris: Maisonneuve et Larose.

Crawford, John 1820, *History of the Indian Archipelago*, vol 2. Edinburgh: Constable.

Daeng Mangemba, Hamzah 1956, *Kenallah Sulawesi Selatan*. Jakarta-Indonesia: Timun Mas.

Daeng Patunru, Abd. Razak 1983, *Sejarah Gowa*. Ujung Pandang-Indonesia: Yayasan Kebudayaan Sulawesi Selatan di Makassar.

Departemen Pendidikan dan Kebudayaan Bidang Penelitian dan Pengkajian Kebudayaan Sulawesi Selatan La Galigo 1985/1986, *Urupu sulapa' appa, Lontara' Bilang Raja Gowa dan Tallo'* (Makassar Manuscripts: A Diary of the Kings of Gowa and Tallo).

Drewes, G.W.J. 1968, New Light on the Coming of Islam to Indonesia. *BKI* 124(4).

Drewes, G.W.J. and Brakel, L.F. 1986, *The Poems of Hamzah Fansuri*. Bibliotheca Indonesica 26. Dordrecht-Holland: Foris Publications.

Evans, Grant 1993, Hierarchy and Dominance: Class, Status and Caste. *Asia's Cultural Mosaic*. Singapore: Prentice Hall.

Fealy, Greg 1997, Indonesian Politics 1995–1996: The Making of a Crisis. Gavin W. Jones and Terence H. Hull (eds), *Indonesian Assessment: Population and Human Resources*. Canberra, ACT: Research School of Pacific and Asian Studies, The Australian National University and Singapore: Institute of Southeast Asian Studies.

Fischer, Michael M.J. and Abedi, Mehdi 1990, *Debating Muslims: Cultural Dialogues in Postmodernity and Tradition*. Madison, WI: University of Wisconsin Press.

Fox, James J. 1979, Standing in Time and Place: The Structure of Rotinese Historical Narratives. Anthony Reid and David Marr (eds), *Perceptions of the Past in Southeast Asia*. Kuala Lumpur: Heinemann Educational Books (Asia) Ltd.

Fox, James J. and Sather, Clifford 1996, *Origins, Ancestry and Alliance: Explorations in Austronesian Ethnography*. Canberra, ACT: Department of Anthropology, Research School of Pacific and Asian Studies, The Australian National University.

Friedericy, H.J. 1933, *De Standen bij de Boegineezen en Makassaren (Social Ranks of the Bugis-Makassar, South Sulawesi-Indonesia)*. Leiden: Rijksuniversiteit te Leiden.

Gassing, A. Qadir 1975, Tinjauan Syari'at Islam terhadap Tradisi Maulid Masyarakat Cikoang Daerah Kabupaten Takalar. Presentation Paper. Indonesia: IAIN Alauddin Ujung Pandang.

Gaudefroy-Demombynes, Maurice 1961, *Muslim Institutions*. London: George Allen & Unwin Ltd., 3rd Impression.

Geertz, Clifford 1984 (1974), From the native's point of view: on the nature of anthropological understanding. Richard Shweder and Robert LeVine (eds), *Culture Theory: Essays on Mind, Self and Emotion*. London: Cambridge University Press.

_____ 1960, *The Religion of Java*. Chicago: The University Chicago Press.

Gervaise, N. 1971, *An Historical Description of The Kingdom of Macassar in the East Indies*. London: Gregg International Publisher Limited.

Gibb, H.A.R 1957, *Ibn Battuta Travels in Asia and Africa 1325–1354*. London: The Broadway Travellers.

Gilsenan, Michael 1973, *Saint and Sufi in Modern Egypt: An Essay in the Sociology of Religion*. Oxford: Clarendon Press.

Graham, William A. 1983, Islam in the Mirror of Ritual. Richard G. Hovannisian and Speros Vryonis, Jr. (eds), *Islam's Understanding of Itself*. Malibu, California: Udena.

Hamid, Abu 1994, *Syekh Yusuf Makassar: Seorang Ulama, Sufi dan Pejuang*. Indonesia: Yayasan Obor.

Hamka, 1984, *Islam dan Adat Minangkabau*. Jakarta-Indonesia: Pustaka Panjimas.

Hamonic, Gilbert 1985, La Fete du grand Maulid a Cikoang, regard sur une tarekat cite 'shi'ite' en Pays Makassar. *Archipel* 29.

Harvey, Barbara Sillars 1989, Pemberontakan Kahar Muzakkar: dari Tradisi ke DI/TII, Jakarta: Grafiti Pers. (English version, Tradition, Islam and Rebellion: South Sulawesi 1950–1965. Department of Government, Cornell University, 1974, unpublished PhD dissertation) Xerox University Microfilms, Ann Arbor MI.

Hefner, Robert 1993, Islam, State and Civil Society: ICMI and the Struggle For the Indonesian Middle Status level. *Indonesia* 56.

Hisyam, Muhammad 1985, Sayyid-Jawi, studi kasus jaringan sosial di Kampong Cikoang, Kecamatan Mangarabombang, Kabupaten Takalar, Sulawesi Selatan, in Mukhlis Paeni and Kathy Robinson (eds), *Agama dan Realitas Sosial*. Ujung Pandang-Indonesia: Lembaga Penerbitan Universitas Hasanuddin.

Hurgronje, C. Snouck 1906, *De Atjehers (The Achehnese)*. Leyden: E.J. Brill.

Johns, A.H. 1980, From coastal settlement to Islamic school and city: Islamization in Sumatra, the Malay peninsula and Java in James J. Fox (ed), *Indonesia: the Making of a Culture*. Canberra, ACT: Research School of Pacific Studies, The Australian National University.

Juynboll, G.H.A. 1983, *Muslim Traditions: Studies in Chronology, Provenance and Authorship of Early Hadith*. Cambridge, New York: Cambridge University Press.

Kamaruddin, H.D. Mangemba, Parawansa, P. and Mappaseleng, M. 1985. Lontarak Bilang Raja Gowa dan Tallok. (Naskah Makassar) Ujung Pandang: Proyek Penelitian dan Pengkajian Kebudayaan Sulawesi Selatan La Galigo.

Keesing, Roger M. 1975, *Kin Groups and Social Structure*. Fort Worth: Holt, Rinehart and Winston.

_____ 1982. Prologue: Toward a Multidimensional Understanding of Male Initiation. In G.H. Herdt (ed.), *Rituals of Manhood*. Berkeley: University of California Press.

Kern, R.A. 1954, *Catalogus van de Boeginese tot de I La Galigo-cyclus behorende handschriften*. Makassar: Yayasan Matthes

Kipp, Rita Smith and Rodgers, Susan (eds) 1987, *Indonesian Religions in Transition*. Tucson: University of Arizona Press.

Kluckhohn, Clyde 1965, Myths and Rituals: A General Theory, in William Armand Lessa and Evon Zartman Vogt (eds), *Reader in Comparative Religion: an Anthropological Approach*. 2nd ed. NY: Harper and Row.

Knappert, Jan 1961, The Figure of the Prophet Muhammad According to the Popular Literature of the Islamic Peoples. *Swahili* No. 32: 24–31.

Koszinowski, Thomas 1983, Jemen-Demokratische Volksrepublik. *Handbuch der Dritten Welt*, Bd. 6, Hoffman und Campe.

Kraemer, H. and C.A.O. van Nieuwenhuijze 1952, *Agama Islam*. Jakarta-Indonesia: Badan Penerbit Kristen (BPK).

Kreemer, J. 1922–23. *Atjeh,* 2 vols. Leiden: E.J. Brill.

Kurin, Richard 1984, Morality, Personhood, and the Exemplary Life: Popular Conceptions of Muslims in Paradise. B.D. Metcalf (ed), *Moral Conduct and Authority: The Place of Adab in South Asian Islam*. Berkeley and Los Angeles: University of California Press.

Lane, Edward William 1860, *An Account of the Manners and Customs of the Modern Egyptians*. 5th ed. London: John Murray.

Lewis, E.D. 1996, Origin Structures and Precedence in the Social Orders of Tana' Ai and Sikka. James J. Fox and Clifford Sather (eds), *Origins, Ancestry and Alliance: Explorations in Austronesian Ethnography*. Canberra, ACT: Department of Anthropology, Research School of Pacific and Asian Studies, The Australian National University.

Liddle, R. William 1996, Islamic Turn in Indonesia: A Political Explanation. *Journal of Asian Studies* 55: 3, August 1996.

Lombard, Denys 1996, *Nusa Jawa: Silang Budaya. Jaringan Asia. Jilid 2.* (1990, *Le Carrefour Javanais. Essai d'histoire globale. 11. Les reseaux asiatiques*). Jakarta: PT Gramedia Pustaka Utama.

Maeda, N. 1984, Traditionality in Bugis Society. In Maeda, N. and Mattulada (eds), *Transformation of the Agricultural Landscape in Indonesia*. Kyoto: Southeast Asian Studies, Kyoto University.

Makruf, Jamhari, 1995, Visit to a Sacred Tomb. Unpublished MA Thesis. Canberra, ACT: Department of Anthropology and Archaelogy, The Australian National University.

Makdisi, George 1990, *The Rise of Humanism in Classical Islam and the Christian West*. Edinburgh University Press.

Malik, K.H.M. 1997, Upacara Maulid Di Cikoang Ditinjau Dari Segi Hukum Islam. Unpublished Paper. Ujung Pandang-Indonesia.

Manyambeang, Abd. Kadir 1984, *Upacara Tradisional Dalam Kaitannya Dengan Peristiwa Alam Dan Kepercayaan Propinsi Sulawesi Selatan*. Ujung Pandang-Indonesia: Proyek Inventarisasi Dan Dokumentasi Kebudayaan Daerah.

Marzuki, L. 1995, *Siri': Bagian Kesadaran Hukum Rakyat Bugis-Makassar (Sebuah Telaah Filsafat Hukum)*. Ujung Pandang: Hasanuddin University Press.

Matthes, B.F. 1864–1872, *Boeginesche Chrestomathie*. Makassar and Amsterdam: Bijbelgenootschap, Vol. II

_____ 1874, *Boegineesch-Hollandsch Woordenboek*. The Hague: M. Nijhoff.

_____ 1883, *Makassaarsche Chrestomathies*. Ujung Pandang-Indonesia: Bungarampai Makassar.

Mattulada 1976, *Islam in South Sulawesi*. Jakarta-Indonesia: LEKNAS/LIPI.

_____ 1982, *Menyusuri Jejak Kehadiran Makassar Dalam Sejarah*. Ujung Pandang-Indonesia: Hasanuddin University Press.

Meglio, Rita Rosedi 1970, *Arab Trade with Indonesia and the Malay Peninsula from the 8th to the 16th Century*. Philadelphia: Bruno Cassirer and the University of Pennsylvania Press.

Mills, R.F. 1975, The Reconstruction of Proto South Sulawesi. *Archipel* 10.

Mukhlis 1975, Struktur Birokrasi Kerajaan Gowa Jaman Pemerintahan Sultan Hasanuddin 1653–1669. Unpublished BA Thesis. Yogyakarta: Universitas Gadjah Mada.

Nicholson, Reynold A. 1921, *Studies in Islamic Mysticism*. Cambridge: Cambridge University Press.

Noer, Deliar 1973, *The Modernist Muslim Movement in Indonesia 1900–1942*. London and New York: Oxford University Press.

Noorduyn, J. 1956, De Islamisering van Makassar. *BKI* 112.

———— 1961, Some Aspects of Macassar-Bugisese historiography. *Historians of Southeast Asia*. D.G. Hall (ed). London: Oxford University Press.

———— 1965, Origins of South Celebes (Sulawesi) historical writing. Soedjatmoko (ed), *An Introduction to Indonesian Historiography*. Ithaca: Cornell University Press.

Nurdin, M. Idrus, Borahima, Ridwan and Manyambeang, A. Kadir 1977/1978: *Laporan Penelitian Tentang Maulid Cikoang: Sebagai Salah Satu Bentuk Kebudayaan Spesifik Tradisional Di Sulawesi Selatan*. Ujung Pandang-Indonesia: Hasanuddin University Project Research.

Patji, Abdur Rachman 1991, The Arabs of Surabaya: A Study of Sociocultural Integration. Unpublished MA thesis. Canberra, ACT: The Australian National University.

Pelras, Christian 1975, 'Célèbes-Sud: Fiche signalétique.' *Archipel* 10.

———— 1985, Religion, Tradition and Dynamics of Islamization in South Sulawesi. *Archipel* 29.

———— 1996, *The Bugis: The Peoples of South-East Asia and the Pacific*. England: Blackwell Publishers, Oxford University Press.

Radcliffe-Brown, A.R. (1950) 1971, Dowry and Bridewealth. Jack Goody (ed), *Kinship: Selected Readings*. England: Penguin Books Ltd.

Raffles, Thomas Standford 1817, *The History of Java*. Volume 1. London: Black, Parbury and Allen.

Reid, Anthony (1988) 1993, *Southeast Asia in the Age of Commerce 1450–1680*, 2 vols. New Haven and London: Yale University Press.

Reid, Anthony and Reid, Helen, 1988, *South Sulawesi*. Berkeley: Periplus Press.

Renaud, E. 1984, Histoir de la pensée religieuse au Yémen. J. Chelhod (ed), *L'Arabie du Sud*, Tome II. Paris: Maisonneuve et Larose.

Rippin, Andrew (1950) 1990, *Muslims: their Religious Beliefs and Practices*. London and New York: Routledge.

Robinson, Kathryn. 1996, Traditions of House Construction in South Sulawesi. *Kumpulan Makalah Seminar Internasional Sejarah, Kebudayaan dan Masyarakat Sulawesi Selatan 16–17 Desember 1996*, Ujung Pandang-Indonesia: Arsip Nasional Wilayah Propinsi Sulawesi Selatan-South Sulawesi.

Robinson, Kathryn and Paeni, Mukhlis (eds) 1998. *Living Through Histories: Culture History and Social Life in South Sulawesi*. Canberra, Research School of Pacific and Asian Studies, The Australian National University.

Roff, William R. 1964, 'The Malayo-Muslim World of Singapore at the Close of the Nineteenth Century.' *Journal of Asian Studies* 24 (1).

Röttger-Rössler 1989, *Rang und Ansehen bei den Makassar von Gowa (Sud-Sulawesi, Indonesien)*. Berlin: Dietrieh Reimer Verlag.

Safwan, Mardanas and Kutoyo, Sutrisno 1981, *Sejarah Pendidikan Daerah Sulawesi Selatan*. Ujung Pandang-Indonesia: Departemen Pendidikan Dan Kebudayaan Proyek Inventarisasi Dan Dokumentasi Kebudayaan Daerah.

Schimmel, Annemarie 1985, *And Muhammad is His Messenger: The Veneration of the Prophet in Islamic Piety*. Chapel Hill: University of North Carolina Press.

Serjeant, R.B. 1981, 'Hud and Other Pre-Islamic Prophets of Hadramawt. [Reprinted from Le Museon, Vol. 62, pp. 121–179] in *Studies in Arabian History and Civilisation*. London: Variorum Reprints.

Shihab, Alwi 1995, *The Muhammadiyah Movement and Its Controversy With Christian Mission in Indonesia*. PhD thesis, Temple University. Photocopy, Ann Arbor, Mich: University Microfilm.

Sila, Muhammad Adlin 1994, Status Hukum Mahar Dalam Perkawinan Menurut Adat Di Kabupaten Gowa Ditinjau Dari Hukum Islam. Unpublished BA thesis. Ujung Pandang-Indonesia: Fakultas Syari'ah IAIN Alauddin.

Skeat, Walter William 1967, *Malay Magic: Being an Introduction to the Folklore and Popular Religion of the Malay Peninsula*. New York: Dover.

Soedjatmoko et al. (eds) 1965, *An Introduction to Indonesian Historical Writing*. Ithaca: Cornell University Press.

Thontowi, Jawahir 1997, *Law and Custom in Makassar Society: The Interaction of Local Custom and the Indonesian Legal System in Dispute Resolution*. Department of Anthropology, University of Western Australia.

Tibbets, G.R. 1957, Early Muslim Traders in South East Asia. *Journal of the Royal Asiatic Society,* Malayan Branch. 30 (1).

van de Berg, L.W.C. 1886, *Le Hadhramaut et les Colonies Arabes dans L'Archipel Indien*. Indonesian Netherlands Cooperation in Islamic Studies (INIS-University of Leiden). Batavia: Impremerie du Gouverement.

Waterson, Roxana 1989, Islam in Transition (Reviews). *Journal of Southeast Asian Studies*. 20 (2): 114–116.

Werbner, Pnina 1990, *The Migration Process: Capital, Gifts and Offerings among British Pakistanis*. Oxford: Berg Publishers.

Westermarck, Edward Alexander 1926, *Ritual and Belief in Morocco*. 2 vols. London: Macmillan.

Woodward, Mark 1989, *Islam in Java: Normative Piety and Mysticism in the Sultanate of Yogyakarta*. Tucson: University of Arizona Press.

Zainal Abidin, Andi 1971, Notes on the Lontara' as Historical Sources. *Indonesia* 12.

Zainuddin, Ailsa 1968, *A Short History of Indonesia*. Melbourne: Cassell Australia.

Magazines

Inside Indonesia, Edition No. 52 October 1997.

Tiras, Edition No. 52/26 January 1998.

Ummat, Edition No. 9/15 September 1997.

www.ingramcontent.com/pod-product-compliance
Lightning Source LLC
Chambersburg PA
CBHW060947170426
43197CB00031B/2985